Brazil's New
Agrarian Reform

PRAEGER SPECIAL STUDIES IN
INTERNATIONAL ECONOMICS AND DEVELOPMENT

Brazil's New Agrarian Reform

AN EVALUATION OF ITS PROPERTY CLASSIFICATION AND TAX SYSTEMS

Armin K. Ludwig
Harry W. Taylor

FREDERICK A. PRAEGER, Publishers
New York • Washington • London

The purpose of the Praeger Special Studies is to make specialized re-search monographs in U.S. and international economics and politics available to the academic, business, and government communities. For further information, write to the Special Projects Division, Frederick A. Praeger, Publishers, 111 Fourth Avenue, New York, N.Y. 10003.

FREDERICK A. PRAEGER, PUBLISHERS
111 Fourth Avenue, New York, N.Y. 10003, U.S.A.
5, Cromwell Place, London S.W.7, England

Published in the United States of America in 1969
by Frederick A. Praeger, Inc., Publishers

Library of Congress Catalog Card Number: 72-93867

Printed in the United States of America

FOR MARTHA AND MARIELLA

PREFACE

If ever a work evolved, this one did. Through
1965 and 1966 each author was independently and un-
beknown to the other studying the structure of São
Paulo State agriculture and its inter-censal changes.
Based on the Brazilian agricultural censuses of 1950
and 1960, these investigations were underwritten by the
Colgate University Research Council, Canada Council,
and the University of Western Ontario. When the
researchers finally pooled their efforts, they sought
to isolate a nonfrontier, near-urban region in which
the most radical inter-censal changes indicating capitalization of agriculture had taken place. The Bragança
Paulista physiographic zone, forty miles due north
of the capital city of São Paulo State, was chosen.
At this point the researchers turned to the field
to ask who had invested in this capitalization and
why—which decision-makers had perceived the opportunity to gain by capitalizing their land.

The Brazilian field work, begun in 1967, was
supported by Canada Council and, in the United
States, by the Social Science Research Council, with
additional support for internal transportation provided by the Agricultural Development Council. The
researchers knew that their task of finding inves-
tors would be eased considerably if they had access
to the detailed questionnaires filled out by all
landholders during the Great Land Inventory of 1966.
The Brazilian Institute of Agrarian Reform (IBRA) in
Rio de Janeiro had these data printed out on cards
for each of Brazil's 3.5 million rural holdings.
Access to the Rio copies would have been long
delayed, except that with the generous help of
officials and employees in the Bragança Paulista
municipal offices, the authors were able to micro-
film these cards for all of the farms in Bragança
Paulista município (county). The information on
each card pertained to economic, social, size, and
location characteristics of the holding, but a good
deal of the data were undecipherable. IBRA

quantified and codified questionnaire information in
order to classify and tax a property according to a
vast, complex system set up by the Land Statute of
November 30, 1964, the basis for Brazil's new agrarian reform. This system's impact on every Brazilian rural holding and thus on the country as a
whole was intended to be great and expected to
intensify. For this reason, the researchers felt
that describing and analyzing the structure, function, and logic of this system and employing the
Bragança Paulista data as a case study in its
application would be their most meaningful contribution to an understanding of the future Brazilian
rural environment. The present work is the result
of this decision.

     Many individuals in the United States, Brazil,
and Canada gave vital support to this research.
Professors John Augelli, Robert Carmin, and Vincent
Barnett were instrumental in helping the authors
obtain financing for the Brazil field work. In
Brazil, Adolfo Kreimer, chief of the Taxation and
Cadastral section of IBRA, was particularly help-
ful, as were Senhors Isidoro and Cesar in the same
office. Many others in the Rio headquarters of
IBRA also supplied aid. Maria Antonia Mucci, chief
of the Department of Industrial Production of the
São Paulo State Department of Statistics aided
immensely the search for statistical information.

     Later, in Canada and the United States,
Professor Robert McDaniel advised on the statistical
parts and Robert Carmin read critically the first
chapter. Diane Coleman helped to prepare the
bibliography, and Arliene Slate typed the tables
and figures. The authors, however, assume full
responsibility for all the factual and conceptual
parts of this work, including any and all errors
contained therein.

CONTENTS

ix

CONTENTS

LIST OF TABLES

LIST OF FIGURES

LIST OF ABBREVIATIONS

AYF   Agricultural Yields Factor

AF   Administrative Factor

BF   Bookkeeping Factor

CD   Coefficient of Dimension

CEY   Coefficient of Economic Yields

CL   Coefficient of Location

CNs   Contract Note, sharecropper

CNt   Contract Note, tenant

Cr$ Old Cruzeiro

CSC   Coefficient of Social Conditions

DAF   Difficulty of Access Factor

DAS   Difficulty of Access Score

EF   Education Factor

ER   Empresa rural

EYF   Economic Yields Factor

FPN   Family Participation Note

HSF   Habitation and Sanitation Factor

IBGE   Instituto Brasileiro de Geografia e Estatistica (Brazilian census bureau)

IBRA   Brazilian Institute of Agrarian Reform

IF   Investment Factor

INDA   Instituto Nacional de Desenvolvimento Agrícola

Lat.   Latifundio

Min.   Minifundio

NCr$	New Cruzeiro, adopted in 1966, equal to 1,000 Old Cruzeiros (U.S.$0.25)
OFLS	Owner-Family-Laborer Score
OPN	Owner Participation Note
RAF	Reliability of Access Factor
RAS	Reliability of Access Score
RNt	Rent Note
SHS	Sharecropper Score
SNs	Share Note
TS	Tenant Score
WLN	Wage Labor Note
UF	Utilization Factor

Brazil's New Agrarian Reform

CHAPTER **1** PROGRESS THROUGH ORDER:
BRAZIL'S APPROACH TO
RURAL CHANGE

Backwardness in Brazilian agriculture poses an increasingly serious threat to continued economic expansion of the country. Brazilian leaders have focused on the rural decision-making base as the strategic variable in the failure of agriculture to keep pace with the needs of its rapidly-growing urban-industrial counterpart. Many of the people making land-use decisions hold parcels too small to reach adequate scales of production. Others hold parcels too large to encourage an intensity of use consistent with optimum input-output relationships. Still others are incapable of effective allocation of agricultural resources because of their value systems or lack of skills. The composite of individual decisions made within this context results in low agricultural production and low incomes in the rural areas and high prices for agricultural commodities in the cities, conditions that reverberate through the economy to slow economic development. Industry is hampered by the low level of effective demand created by low rural incomes at the same time that high prices for limited agricultural raw materials and for wage goods contribute to high prices for industrial products. In addition, rural poverty has serious social and political implications. It is no longer a condition to be tolerated in the light of the national insecurity and potential political instability it breeds.

The Land Statute (Estatuto da Terra) which became the law of the land on November 30, 1964, grew out of the need to alter the rural decision-making base. It is the logical and highly elaborated extension of Article 147 of the 1946 Federal Constitution which enables the President of the Republic to decree land-reform measures. The Statute has as its prime goals the shaping of an

3

agricultural system consistent with continuing economic expansion and the promotion of economic and
social justice in the rural environment.

BRAZILIAN APPROACHES TO AGRARIAN REFORM

The Land Statute is a complex, fifty-three-
page document, which, although not organized exactly
along the following lines, reflects its framers'
concerns with these eight approaches to agrarian
reform:
1. commitment to private enterprise;
2. necessity for government intervention;
3. creation of instruments to implement agricultural change on privately held properties;
4. establishment of performance norms for
such properties;
5. isolation of remedial-action regions in
which numerous properties fail to meet these norms;
6. planning and implementation of agricultural
colonies to absorb the potential surplus population;
7. creation of agencies to administer the
above programs;
8. setting up of the Land Inventory.

The first principle of Brazilian agrarian reform is that exploitation of the agricultural resources of the nation is to be carried out within a
context of private enterprise. This principle seems
to be based upon either a moral commitment or an
unfavorable assessment, objective or subjective, of
the performance of agriculture in the more highly
collectivized economies of the world. Both of these
factors are probably involved. In any case, the
political realities of the nation tend to militate
against any other point of departure for reform.

On the other hand, unrestricted private enterprise has not resulted in effective use of the rural
land. Accordingly, private ownership and exploitation of land in the future is to be contingent upon
effective use of land toward attainment of the economic and social values of the nation. This principle proceeds from two notions: (1) that the
potential contribution of the agricultural sector
of the economy is far greater than its current performance seems to indicate; (2) that this potential
can be far more fully realized through strong governmental intervention. In fact, the gap between

potential and actual is judged to be so great that
an almost complete overhaul of the agrarian sector
is deemed necessary.

This reshaping of the agricultural sector is
to be achieved through the application of two basic
tools:differential land taxation and abridgment of
the right to private property. Properties that are
deemed too large or too small, or not properly ex-
ploited, are subject to limits on their disposal or
to expropriation. In order to avoid excessive use
of this economically expensive and politically
dangerous weapon, the law permits each owner to
make voluntary adjustments to correct these characteristics. If such adjustments are not made, expropriation is to be carried out. Excessively
large properties are to be subdivided, those which
are too small are to be consolidated, and the im-
properly used are to be placed under the ownership
of operators who presumably are willing and able to
bring the land into more desirable forms of use.

Differential taxation is an added incentive
for adjustment on the part of propertyholders.
This spur applies more to large and ineffectively
operated holdings than to small ones. In general,
larger and more poorly used properties are taxed
more heavily than other holdings.

In an ideal sense, then, the Brazilian Government wants rural property owners to make adjustments in the size and operation of their holdings
that will bring them to higher levels of performance. Presumably, if they do not make such adjustments voluntarily, they can be coerced into doing
so, or can be replaced by owners who will. But
what is the model to be emulated? And how are the
undesirable to be recognized? The answers to these
questions require a quantitative definition of size
and performance norms. From the government's point
of view, a property is desirable only if it meets
clearly defined quantitive standards of size and
operation. All other holdings are undesirable.
Although the Land Statute establishes a system of
classification in which four types of holdings are
recognized, the government regards Brazilian holdings as of basically two kinds: the desirable,
called empresas rurais; and the undesirable, categorized as minifundios, latifundios by size, and

latifundios by use.[1] Any property in any of the
last three categories lies under the threat of expropriation or abridgment of free disposal.

At the same time a tax is levied on all properties.   The rate at which each property is taxed
depends upon its size, location, input-output
relationships, and social conditions. Quantitative
assessment of these characteristics results in four
coefficients whose product is the basis for calculation of the tax. Any propertyholder, then, can
subsequently reduce his tax rate by modifying these
characteristics, and in so doing may alter a coefficient sufficiently to change the property's
status from undesirable to desirable.

The Statute systems of classification and taxation are to be applied from the outset to all
rural properties, yet an immediate, far-reaching
transformation of the agricultural sector of the
economy is not possible. There are approximately
3.5 million rural properties in the country, but
fewer than 10 per cent have been classified
empresas rurais. The human resources and capital
necessary to bring all substandard holdings, or
even half of them, to prescribed norms would be
staggering. Nor is such an immediate transformation necessarily desirable. One can imagine the
strains in the Brazilian economy and social fabric
if all these farm units were suddenly brought within
these prescribed norms.

Brazilian leaders recognize that the agricultural problems and resulting economic pressures and
social tensions are more acute in some areas than
in others. Consequently, the Statute calls for the
establishment of priority areas where corrective
measures can be instituted immediately.

Although it is readily apparent that a very
small percentage of the people own most of the
land, excessive subdivision of the remainder is an
acute Brazilian problem. Over 2.5 million properties in the country have been classified minifundios. If a large number of these are to be
consolidated, as called for by the Statute, many
farm families will be uprooted from their current
homes. Consequently, alternative employment must
be provided. One logical source of such employment is the urban-industrial sector. But urban
areas are already being called upon to accept far

more migrants than their capacity permits them to
absorb in an effective manner. In order to dampen
the rural-to-urban flow of people, colonization of
potentially productive lands in the interior is
seen as a necessary counterpart of land consol-
idation in the already developed areas.

Land-reform legislation, of one sort or
another, is to be found among the laws of almost
every country in Latin America, but in only a few
cases has this legislation been applied. The reasons for this lack of execution are manifold, but
at least one significant factor has been the failure
to create strong and unfettered agencies charged
with the responsibility for administering the laws.
The Brazilian Land Statute creates two organiza-
tions: The Instituto Brasileiro de Reforma Agrária
(IBRA) and the Instituto Nacional de Desenvolvimento Agrícola (INDA). In the light of recent
(February, 1969) disclosures of irregularities in
IBRA, it remains to be seen how strong and unfettered that agency really is.[2] Currently, IBRA is
the more strategic of these agencies in that it is
charged with the classification and taxation of
properties, expropriation of properties in priority
areas, and general application of the regulations
of the Statute. INDA is charged, basically, with
the shaping of long-run agricultural development
policy, but is also expected to participate, along
with IBRA, in the design and implementation of
colonization schemes.

THE GREAT LAND INVENTORY

Much had to be known about any landholding in
order for it to be fit into the complicated system
of classification directed by the Land Statute. To
this end, and pursuant to Article 46 of the Land
Statute, IBRA conducted Brazil's first comprehen-
sive land inventory in late 1965 and early 1966.
Each propertyowner (or a legal proxy) was required
to purchase and fill out a four-page questionnaire
about his property. Where called for, he also had
to fill out annexes regarding sharecroppers and
tenants and to supply information on additional
property holdings in Brazil. (The questionnaire,
translated into English, is found in Appendix A.)

For the purpose of dramatizing the inventory
and mobilizing participation in it, Semanas da

Terra(Land Weeks) were set up in various parts of
the country. Response was good, considering the
difficulty of communication and travel in the vast
interior of Brazil, no doubt improved by the fact
that an owner had to make the declaration in order
to obtain a Cadastral Certificate, without which he
would be unable to obtain financing or credit, get
a guarantee of minimum prices in sales of his produce, request any form of technical assistance, or
dismember, rent, sell, mortgage, or otherwise
transfer his property.

An owner (or proxy) who was not able to fill
out the questionnaire during Land Week could do so
without penalty until December 31, 1966, in the
office of the município (county) where his property
was located. By May, 1967, more than 3.4 million
questionnaires had been returned, a figure that
approximates IBRA's estimate of the total number of
rural properties in Brazil.

The accuracy of the inventory can easily be
called into question. Many errors doubtless resulted from the small farmer's ignorance of the
details of his own land, and others from misinter-
pretation of or inattention to details on the
questionnaire. Some inaccuracies may, of course,
have been deliberate falsifications. Since the
Land Statute requires an inventory every five years,
in addition to improving the system of data collection, IBRA may well find a way to check the accuracy of a large percentage of the responses. But
this inventory, as it stands, is the reality with
which IBRA had to work. Punched on cards and
programmed through a computer, these were the data
that determined a property's place in the classification system and its tax rate.

Summarizing, then, the framers of the Statute
held that property ought to remain in private
hands, but that the government has the duty to
intervene in the public interest to try to force
internal changes on all properties in the direction
of Statute norms. The Statute specifies that this
can best be done by increasing the weight of a
property's taxes in direct proportion to its distance below the norms, and, for properties beyond
specified distances below these norms, by abridging
the owner's right to free disposal or by outright
expropriation and the granting of decision-making
control to another person. The Statute orders an

inventory of Brazilian rural properties to determine how far each holding lies from the norms, and
a colonization program to absorb in the rural sector
those displaced or dispossessed by the application
of pressures and penalties. It creates new agencies,
separate and apart from all existing ones, and
charges them with implementing these approaches to
an agrarian reform.

Brazil's approach to land reform raises the
following major questions:
1. How much rural decision-making can be left
in private hands?
2. How much should be forced by direct government intervention?
3. Can such instruments as taxation, abridgment, and expropriation bring about the desired
economic and social changes?
4. How restrictive or how lenient should the
norms be to accomplish the desired changes?
5. Where and why are the priority areas to be
set up?
6. Will agricultural colonies aid in solving
present and future agrarian problems and where will
they work best?
7. How responsive are IBRA and INDA to their
charges, how free are they of old political ties
and solutions, and do they have the funds, power,
personnel, and will to carry out their mandates?
8. Is the Land Inventory accurate and useful
as constituted and what does it say about existing
Brazilian rural reality?

OUTLINE OF THE STUDY

The foci of this work are the rural property-
classification system and tax system, the cores of
Brazilian agrarian reform set up by the Statute and
articulated by subsequent decrees. The first five
chapters of this study examine the structure,
function, goals, rationales, and logic, not only
of these systems' end products, but also of each of
their several elements, making use of Inventory data
from properties in Bragança Paulista município [3] to
exemplify and characterize these elements and their
results. These chapters then apply selected
Inventory data to all of Brazil's 214 physiographic
zones to measure regional variation in existing

FIGURE 1

The Structure of the Monograph

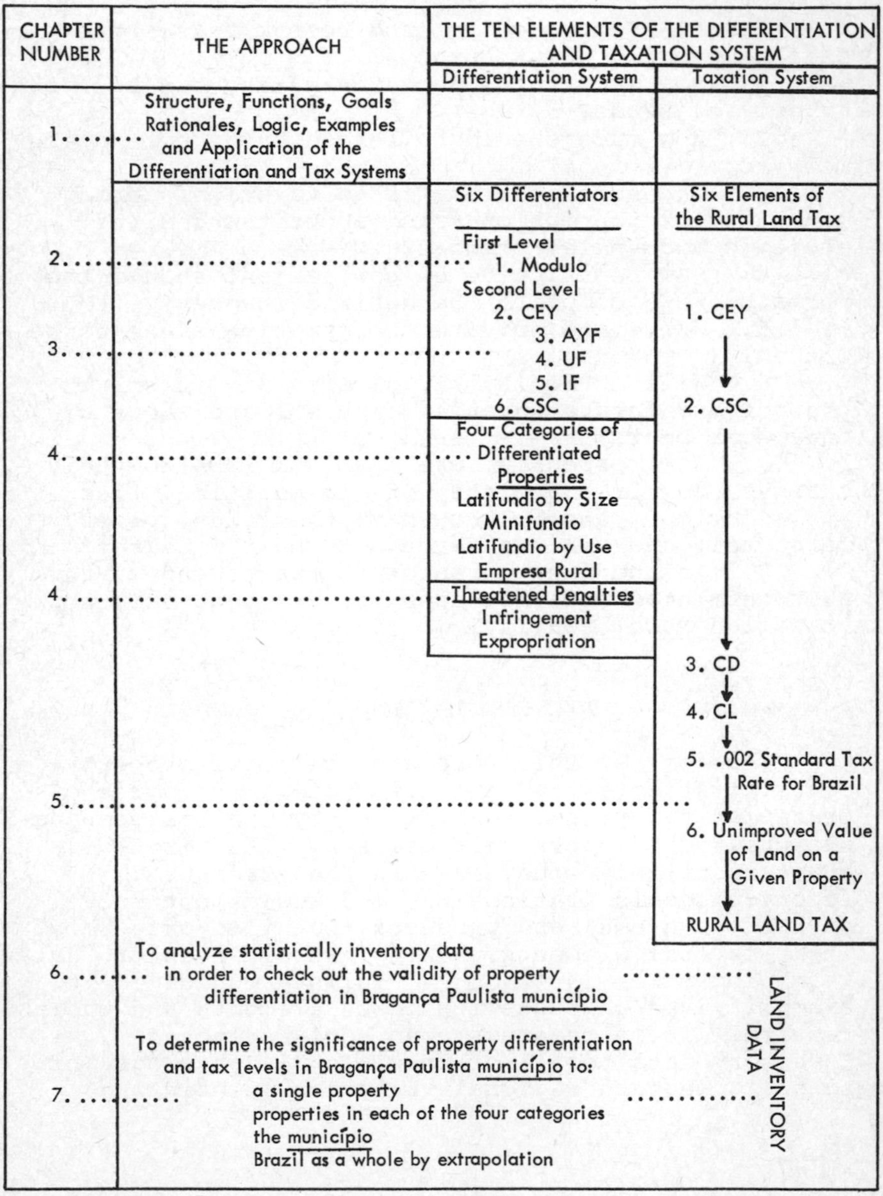

CHAPTER NUMBER	THE APPROACH	THE TEN ELEMENTS OF THE DIFFERENTIATION AND TAXATION SYSTEM	
		Differentiation System	Taxation System
1.........	Structure, Functions, Goals Rationales, Logic, Examples and Application of the Differentiation and Tax Systems		
2..............................		Six Differentiators First Level ··· 1. Modulo Second Level 2. CEY 3. AYF 4. UF 5. IF 6. CSC	Six Elements of the Rural Land Tax 1. CEY ↓ 2. CSC
3........................			
4..............................		Four Categories of ···· Differentiated Properties Latifundio by Size Minifundio Latifundio by Use Empresa Rural	
4..............................		·Threatened Penalties Infringement Expropriation	
			3. CD ↓ 4. CL ↓ 5. .002 Standard Tax Rate for Brazil
5...............................			··· 6. Unimproved Value of Land on a Given Property ↓ RURAL LAND TAX
6...........	To analyze statistically inventory data in order to check out the validity of property differentiation in Bragança Paulista município ··············		LAND INVENTORY DATA
7.............	To determine the significance of property differentiation and tax levels in Bragança Paulista município to: a single property properties in each of the four categories the município Brazil as a whole by extrapolation ··············		

10

rural reality and in some of the key elements of
the agrarian reform system. In doing this, these
chapters provide more than partial answers to the
first four questions.

Questions six and seven cannot be fully an-
swered by this study, since it does not focus
directly on agricultural colonization nor on the
administrative structures of IBRA and INDA, but it
necessarily touches upon those questions because
they are so closely related to the operation of
the property-classification and taxation systems.

The work is not concerned with analyzing the
Land Inventory, although it does draw heavily upon
Inventory data for Braganca Paulista município.
Chapter 6 employs these data to test, statistically,
the validity of the Statute-IBRA classification
system, and in Chapter 7 these data are also used
to determine what the assessment and collection of
the tax actually mean to Bragança properties, to
the município and its rural environment, and, by
extension, to the Brazilian nation.
Figure 1 lays out the complete structure of
this book.

                         NOTES

1. Since these terms will be used so often in
this book, they will not be italicized in further
use.

2. Paul Montgomery, "Brazil Continues to
Widen Control," New York Times (February 28, 1969),
p. 5.

3. The município (a political unit roughly
equivalent to an American county) of Bragança
Paulista is located in the state of São Paulo about
40 miles due north of the capital city.

CHAPTER **2** FIRST-LEVEL
DIFFERENTIATION OF
RURAL PROPERTIES

The Brazilian Land Statute calls for the classification of rural properties into four basic types: (1) empresas rurais; (2) latifundios by use; (3) minifundios; (4) latifundios by size. The first distinction between these types is that of size. Minifundios are too small and latifundios by size too large to effectively contribute to the accomplishment of Brazilian economic and social goals, while empresas rurais and latifundios by use fall within an acceptable size range. The last two types are distinguished from each other on the basis of performance criteria. Since minifundios and latifundios by size are defined on the basis of size regardless of their performance, size is referred to here as the first-level differentiator and performance as the second-level differentiator.

THE MODULO CONCEPT

Central to the system of classification at both levels is the concept of the modulo. A modulo is defined in Article Four, Paragraph II, of the Land Statute as that quantity of land which is capable of absorbing all the labor of four working adults and of supporting them at a standard of living which is consistent with the overall goals of economic progress and social justice. This concept recognizes that two parcels of land equal in size may have different productive capacities due to differences in physical qualities and location near or far from market. A modulo, then, is a unit of measure that varies from place to place but that always has the same meaning in economic terms. Thus the size of a specific property can be stated in terms of modulos once its productive capacity is known.

The commitment of this concept immediately raises a hugh technical problem:that of evaluating the productive capacity of each property in the country. Such a task was recognized by Edgard Texeira Leite, one of the leaders in Brazilian land-reform thought, as impossible in the short run and, because of changing economic and technical conditions, as almost useless in the long run.[1] Here the Statute makes two compromises. First, the physical quality of the land is to be inferred from the use the land is being put to by its current owner.(The wisdom exercised by the owner in selecting his land use is assessed, though indirectly, at the second level of differentiation.) Secondly, the Statute charges IBRA with establishing standard modulo sizes for differing land use types by regions of market potential.[2]

For the purpose of establishing regional types, the 214 physiographic zones in the country set up by the Conselho Nacional de Geografia were grouped by IBRA into nine classes, based on their population potential and proximity to an urban nucleus (Figures 2 and 3).[3] Classes A_1, A_2, and A_3 comprise all physiographic zones with population potentials greater than 100,000 persons per kilometer. Classes B_1, B_2, and B_3 are made up of zones with a potential of from 60,000 to 100,000. Classes C_1 and C_2 include zones whose population potential is 30,000 to 60,000 persons per kilometer. All other zones are designated D.

The subdivisions of A, B, and C are based upon the incidence of various-sized urban concentrations within the zones. A_1 and B_1 contain at least one urban nucleus of more than 500,000 inhabitants. A_2 and B_2 contain at least one urban center with a population larger than 50,000. A_3 and B_3 contain no urban nuclei over 50,000, but are contiguous to a zone that contains an urban center of 5,000 persons or more.

In addition to these classifications, the Statute establishes six major land-use types. Arranged in estimated descending order of their potential for generating income per unit area, these categories are: (1) market gardening; (2) perennial-crop farming; (3) annual crop cultivation; (4) intensive grazing; (5) extensive grazing; (6) forest exploitation. Table 1 shows the nine zone classes and six land-use types arranged in

FIGURE 2

Hypothetical Map of the Nine
Physiographic Zone Classes
(Based on population potential and
proximity to urban nuclei)

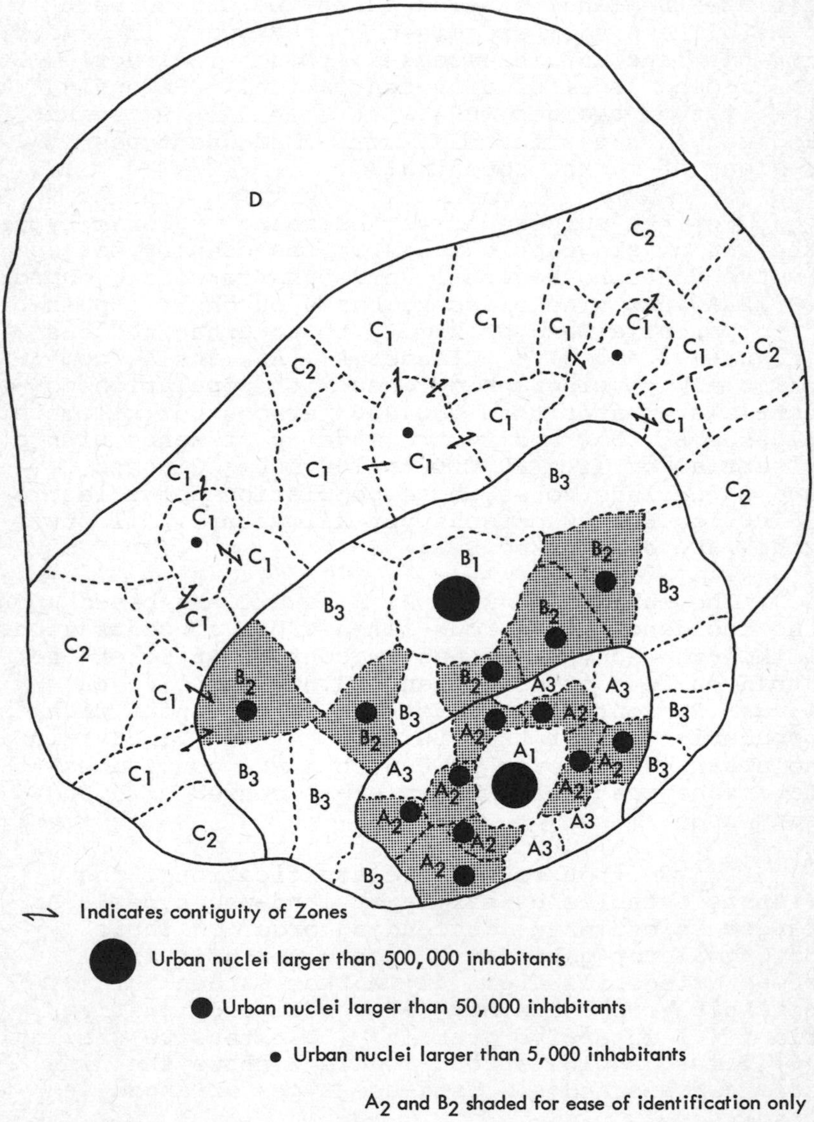

⤵ Indicates contiguity of Zones

⬤ Urban nuclei larger than 500,000 inhabitants

● Urban nuclei larger than 50,000 inhabitants

• Urban nuclei larger than 5,000 inhabitants

A_2 and B_2 shaded for ease of identification only

14

FIGURE 3

The Nine Classes Based on Population
Potential and Proximity to Urban Nuclei and Which
Are Applicable to Brazil's 214 Physiographic Zones

| | Population Potential | | | Incidence of Urban Nuclei | | | |
| | | | | Zone contains urban nucleus of: | | Zone contiguous to one with urban nucleus of: | |
	More than 100,000	100,000 60,000	60,000 30,000	More than 500,000	More than 50,000	More than 50,000	More than 5,000
A_1	X			X			
A_2	X				X		
A_3	X					X	
B_1		X		X			
B_2		X			X		
B_3		X				X	
C_1			X				
C_2			X				X
D None of these							

matrix form. IBRA's problem was to complete the
matrix by determining a value, in hectares, for
each zone--the "Standard modulo size" for each kind
of zone and land use.

   IBRA's method for deriving these values is
quite complex. Simply stated, it involves three
steps: (1) determination of the level of income
that is adequate support for four working adults;
(2) estimation of the amount of income that can be
generated per hectare under the various land uses
in the different zone; (3) division of the necessary income by the estimated income-generating
capacity per hectare for a given land use and zone.
Simply stated:

   necessary income = adequate support for four
                      adults
   number of hectares = necessary income/estimated
                        income-generating capacity

   In deriving necessary income levels, IBRA found
guidance in Brazilian labor legislation. Minimum
salaries have been set for years in Brazil by federal law, according to regions that have a rough
equivalence to the IBRA zones. To be consistent
with this legislation, for self-employed farmers
and farm families, IBRA decided that a modulo must
be capable of generating income equivalent to at
least four minimum salaries in its zone. But labor
is not the only factor of production; land and capital are also used in the productive process. In
recognition of this fact, IBRA adds a return of 15
per cent to each of these two factors to the income
that a modulo must be capable of producing. For this
purpose, IBRA postulates that land is capitalized at
50 per cent of its unimproved value. Therefore the
total value of the unimproved land is assumed to be
150 per cent of its unimproved value and a return of
15 per cent to each factor means a total return of
22.5 per cent to the capital and land. Besides
these returns to labor, capital, and land, IBRA adds
one further requirement for a modulo--income to cover
social services such as housing and education for
the property's occupants. Traditionally, under
the patrão system, landholders in Brazil have had
the responsibility for providing these services to
laborers, tenants, sharecroppers, and dependent
children on their properties, and IBRA feels that
a modulo should generate an additional 40 per cent

of the four minimum salaries so that these responsibilities can be met. (This provision almost seems irrelevant in the case of a family-owned and -operated farm, but these services still must be provided for at least the owner's family.) To be a modulo, then, the income that a unit of land must be capable of generating is equal to 1.6 times four annual minimum salaries in the zone, plus 15 per cent of the combined value of the property's unimproved land and its fixed capital--that is, 22.5 per cent of its improved value. And since minimum salaries vary spatially, a modulo value was calculated for each zone class.

Estimates of the second set of values, for productive capacity per hectare, were based on studies of crop yields on sample holdings throughout Brazil, most of which were made prior to the enactment of the Statute. A partial list of the studies used is included in Appendix B. Broader representation may have been desirable, but time was deemed of high priority at the outset of the program. In order to eliminate some of the inequities of the present estimates, IBRA is making revisions of standard modulo sizes as additional studies permit. In fact, in some cases, standard modulo sizes have already been revised to the level of the município rather than that of the physiographic zone.

The crop yield per hectare extrapolated from these studies is multiplied by the minimum price for the pertinent crop in the area in question to yield an estimate of gross-income capacity. Expected net income is then calculated by subtracting direct costs, except for labor costs, from the gross-income capacity. Since standard modulo sizes are applicable to land use types rather than specific crops or animal products within each land-use category.

The standard modulo sizes in Table 1 were derived by dividing the required modulo incomes by income-generating capacity per hectare for a given land use in a given zone.

$$\text{Standard modulo size}_{ij} = \frac{(1.6 \times 4 \times \text{minimum salary}_i) + (.225 \times \text{postulated value of improved land})}{\text{income-generating capacity per hectare}_{ij}}$$

(Where i refers to the zones (rows) and j to the land use types (columns).)

Since there are nine kinds of zone and six land-use
types, 54 standard modulo sizes were calculated.

It is clear that modulo sizes were assumed to
be more closely related to the market potential
(the basis for classifying the zones) than any other
factor. Physical variations within the zones, such
as soil and slope differences, were ignored. This
was without doubt far too great an assumption of
internal uniformity in a physiographic zone, but a
necessary assumption, given the scarcity of time
and resources.

USE OF THE MODULO

Once the land use and zone location of a rural
holding are known, it can be classified on the basis
of the number of farm families that it should be
able to support; that is, on the basis of its size
in modulos rather than its size in simple areal
units, such as hectares. The number of modulos in
a property determines whether it is disqualified
from empresa rural status as either a minifundio or
a latifundio by size. If it has less than one modulo, it is a minifundio. If it contains more than
600 modulos, it is a latifundio by size. As we
shall see later, if it lies between these two limits,
it is either an empresa rural or a latifundio by use.

For greater clarity, let us consider the application of the system to a specific holding. Let us
assume that Senhor João is the sole owner of a
single holding of 300 hectares in Bragança Paulista
physiographic zone in São Paulo state, and that
his property is divided into the following land-use
types:

1.	market gardening	30 hectares
2.	perennial crops	0 hectares
3.	temporary crops	30 hectares
4.	small livestock	20 hectares
5.	large livestock	70 hectares
6.	forestry	0 hectares

Area Useable and Used	150 hectares
Area Useable but Not Used	50 hectares
Total Useable Land	200 hectares
Total Unuseable Land	100 hectares
Total Area of Farm	300 hectares

As a first step in the classification of this holding, we must determine its average modulo size. Then, by dividing the total useable land by this average modulo size, we establish the size of the property in modulos. The average modulo is calculated in the following manner: The holding is in Braganca Paulista physiographic zone, which is classed as A_3. Consulting the A_3 row of Table 1, we find the standard modulo sizes for the six types of land uses. Now if we multiply the area of each type of land use by its respective standard modulo size (for example, 30 hectares in market gardening times 3 hectares) we obtain figures of 90, 600, 440, and 3,500. These are termed partial modular products. Their sum is 4,630 which when divided by the total used area (150 hectares) yields an average modulo equal to 30.8 hectares. This operation is laid out graphically below.

Standard Modulo Sizes For A_3 Zones, in Hectares		João's Total, in Hectares	Partial Modular Product
3 in market gardening	x	30	= 90
20 in temporary crops	x	30	= 600
22 in small livestock	x	20	= 440
50 in large livestock	x	70	= 3,500
		150	4,630/150=30.8

In practice, this figure is rounded to 30 hectares. The total useable land (200 hectares) is then divided by this average modulo of 30 to produce a property size of 6.7 modulos. Since the number of modulos in João's holding lies between 1 and 600, it is neither a minifundio nor a latifundio by size.

LOGIC OF THE MODULO'S STRUCTURE AND USE

The reason for classifying a holding of less than one modulo in size a minifundio is obvious: by definition it is unable to support four adults at standards that are acceptable, given Brazilian agrarian-reform goals.

But the answers to two other questions are not quite so obvious. First, why is 600 a critical figure for modulos? The explanation probably lies in the desire of Brazilian leaders to allow a fairly wide margin for error in classifying properties during early phases of reform. The 600-modulo limit may reflect, as well, a compromise in the face of

TABLE 1

Standard Modulo Sizes in Hectares by
Zone Classes and Types of Land Use

Modulo Zone	Market Gardening (1)	Perennial Crops (2)	Temporary Crops (3)	Small Live-Stock (4)	Large Live-Stock (5)	Forestry (6)	Unused, Use Not Given (7)
A_1	2	10	13	14	30	45	20
A_2	2	13	16	18	40	60	25
A_3	3	15	20	22	50	60	30
B_1	3	16	20	25	50	80	35
B_2	3	20	25	30	60	85	40
B_3	4	25	30	35	70	90	45
C_1	4	30	35	45	90	110	50
C_2	5	35	45	50	110	115	55
C_3	5	40	50	55	110	120	60

Sources: IBRA, Instrucão Especial, 1, (September 15, 1965); Regulamenta for Chapter 1 of Title 1, Section 3 of the Land Statute (March 3, 1965); Regulamenta for Chapter 1 of Title III of the Land Statute (August 26, 1965).

political pressures from large property owners or
tacit assumptions about the relationship between
scales of production and land productivity.

Secondly, why <u>multiply</u> the areas in various
land uses by the ideal modulo values of their types
in order to derive an average modulo size for a
property? Instead, why not <u>divide</u> each area by its
respective standard modulo size--that is, establish
the actual number of modulos in each type of land
use, then add these to determine the modular size of
the property? Applying this simpler, seemingly more
logical method, Joao's farm would have 13.8 modulos:

<u>Crop</u>

market gardening	30/3	=	10.0
annual crops	30/20	=	1.5
small livestock	20/22	=	.9
large livestock	70/50	=	1.4
			13.8 = Total Modulos

IBRA assigns João's property fewer modulos (6.7)
than would this simpler method, and in general allows
more large properties to escape disqualification as
latifundios by size. But at the lower end of the
modulo continuum, the IBRA method tends to push
holdings toward and into the minifundio category.
Consider these actual figures for a property in
Bragança Paulista <u>município</u>:

<u>IBRA Method</u>					<u>Simple Method</u>		
Standard Modulo Size		Hectares			Hectares	Standard Modulo Size	
15	x	3.6	=	54	3.6 / 15		= .24
20	x	7.2	=	144	7.2 / 20		= .36
22	x	4.8	=	105	4.8 / 22		= .22
50	x	9.6	=	480	9.6 / 50		= .19
60	x	3.6	=	210	3.6 / 60		= .06
		28.8		993/28.8=34.4			1.07

Property Modulo = 0.8   Property Modulo = 1.07

IBRA assigns 0.8 modulos, making the holding a minifundio, but the property would not be disqualified
by the simpler method, which gives it 1.1 modulos.

IBRA's method of calculation clearly weakens the
power of Brazilian land reform to disqualify and
break up large properties and strengthens its capacity to disqualify and absorb small holdings. It
is far from clear, however, why IBRA should wish to
do this. None of the highly knowledgeable IBRA
officials with whom the authors discussed the two
methods could offer a rationale for IBRA's more complicated method of determining the modulo.

A property's status as a latifundio by size may
be established either by calculation of its modulos
or automatically. The automatic classification
applies to all properties larger than 72,000 hectares
or more than 600 times the size of the average holding in its physiographic zone.[4] In applying the
modulo criterion, 2.5 million holdings, 76 per cent
of the properties classified, have been declared
minifundios, while 1,740 properties have been
classified as latifundio by size, 600 by modulo
calculation and 1,440 automatically.

IBRA's interest, of course, goes far beyond
size. It is focused just as sharply on the allocation of resources within the agricultural firm.
IBRA expects owners' decisions affecting the use of
their land and the economic and social conditions on
their properties to be consistent with the larger
goals of the nation as expressed in the Statute.
The Coefficient of Economic Yield (CEY) and the
Coefficient of Social Conditions (CSC) have been
set up to measure the effects of these decisions.
Through these coefficients and associated measures,
IBRA hopes to be able to determine which of those
potential empresas rurais (properties not previously
declared minifundios or latifundios by size) are in
fact the rural enterprises sought by Brazilian
agrarian reform and deemed vital to the nation.
Chapters 3 and 4 are devoted to an examination of
these measures in their roles as second-level dif-
ferentiators.

NOTES

1. Edgard Texeira Leite, "O problema da terra
no Brasil," Revista Brasileira de Geografia (abril-
junho, 1959), pp. 127-146.

2. The determination of population potential
use by IBRA is a specific application of the general
models in current use, which are based upon an
analogy between gravity and the potential interac-
tion of population and/or population centers. It
follows the general mathematical formulation:

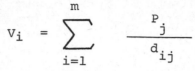

$$V_i = \sum_{i=1}^{m} \frac{P_j}{d_{ij}}$$

where V_i is the population potential at point i,
P_j is the population at point j, and d is the distance between point i and point j. V is always
stated in population per linear measure.

3. For the derivation of these standard modulo
sizes, see IBRA, "Módulo," <u>Cadernos do IBRA</u> (II,1),
p.3.

4. The average-size holding per zone is given
in the <u>Instrucão Especial</u>, 1, September 15, 1965.
In Bragança Paulista the average property has 37
hectares, and 600 times this average would be
22,200 hectares. Brazil's smallest average holding
is 4 hectares in Pindaré zone in the northern state
of Maranhão. Here any property larger than 2,400
hectares (600 x 4) automatically becomes a latifundio by size with a Coefficient of Dimension of
4.5.

CHAPTER THE COEFFICIENT OF
ECONOMIC YIELDS AND ITS
COMPONENTS: FOUR
SECOND-LEVEL CRITERIA

The result of first-level classification is a
grouping of properties into three categories. Properties of less than one modulo are declared minifundios and properties of 601 modulos or more are
declared latifundios by size. The remaining properties must be subjected to further tests before
they may be finally classified as latifundios by
use or empresas rurais. This process of separating
properties of acceptable size into the two classes
mentioned above is referred to here as second-level
differentiation. The five criteria in this differentiation are measures of performance, four related
to economic goals and one to social goals. There
is no order of priority in applying these criteria,
since a property in the proper size range is classified latifundio by use if it does not meet any
one of the standards. A property that meets all
standards is classified as empresa rural.

The problem of describing and explaining this
level of differentiation is complicated by the fact
that one of the criteria, the Coefficient of Economic Yields (CEY) is derived in part from three of
the other criteria: the Agricultural Yields Factor,
the Economic Yields Factor, and the Utilization
Factor. (See Figure 4.) For this reason, only
four economic criteria are treated in this chapter.
The final criterion, the Coefficient of Social Conditions (CSC), is treated in Chapter 4.

THE UTILIZATION FACTOR

The Utilization Factor (UF) is a measure of
the degree to which useable land is actually used.
On the IBRA questionnaire, each rural propertyholder classifies his land according to how much of

it is useable and how much is not. He also indicates how much he actually uses. If the land he
uses is less than 50 per cent of the total useable
land, his property is declared a latifundio by use.
In the CEY formula the value remains in decimal
form, ranging from 0 to 1.0 in units of 0.1 (hun-
dredths are ignored). Our hypothetical Senhor João
in Bragança Paulista would have a UF of 0.7, since
of his 200 useable hectares only 150 (75 per cent,
or 0.7) are actually used. If an owner fails to
indicate the area of useable land, IBRA employs the
total area of his property as the divisor in determining the UF.

THE AGRICULTURAL YIELDS FACTOR

The Agricultural Yields Factor (AYF) is derived
by comparing a property's actual yields per hectare in basic uses, such as those presented in
Table 2 for a Bragança Paulista holding, against
standard yields set by IBRA for these uses (Table 3).
(If an owner fails to indicate on the questionnaire
his basic-use areas and yields, then his AYF becomes the product of his Economic Yields Factor and
his Investment Factor.) Although yield data vary
widely among Brazil's 3.4 million rural properties,
the AYF calculation for each follows that shown in
Table 4 for the Bragança holding. For each basic
use, IBRA's standard minimum yield is subtracted
from the actual yield, and the remainder divided by
the difference between IBRA's standard minimum and
standard good yields. The resulting quotient is
assigned a yield score from Table 5, and this score
is multiplied by the number of hectares devoted to
that use. These weighted yield values are then
added and the sum divided by the total area in basic
uses. The final quotient is the AYF, which ranges
from 0.5 to 1.5.

The AYF reflects the degree to which yields on
a property meet IBRA standards. In a real sense it
is an expression of the level of productivity of
the system employed by the landholder--the higher
the productivity, the greater the AYF. Any potential empresa rural with an AYF below 0.7 is classified as a latifundio by use.

Obviously a series of 0.5 yield scores from
production below IBRA standard minimum yields is
going to produce a 0.5 AYF and make the property

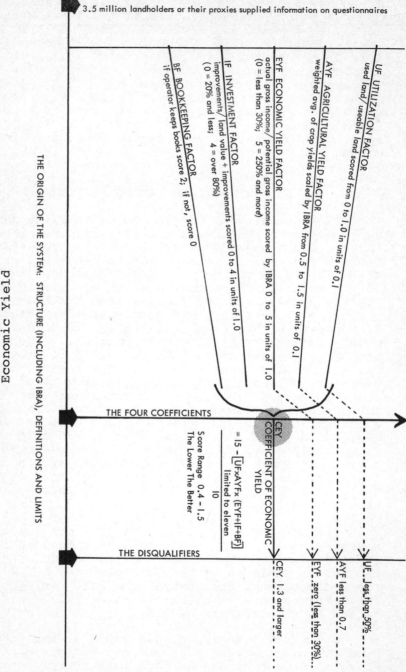

FIGURE 4

Development of the Coefficient of
Economic Yield

TABLE 2

Actual Basic Use Data for
a Bragança Paulista Holding

Use	Area in Hectares	Yield	Yield per Hectare
Coffee	40	27 tons	.6 tons
Beans	10	not 10 per cent of used land[a]	
Tobacco	2	not 10 per cent of used land[a]	
Corn	48	90 tons	1.8 tons
Cattle	108	220 head	2.0 head
Forest[b]	144		
	352		

a No use normally listed by IBRA as basic is considered unless it occupies at least 10 per cent of a property's total land. Nevertheless, its area is added to the total amount of used land on a property..

b In no case is forest considered by IBRA a basic crop, although land in forest is added to the total amount of used land on a property.

TABLE 3

Standard Yields for Basic Land Uses

Uses	Areas of Application	Units	Minimum (a)	Good (b)	Difference (b-a)
Perennial Crops					
Tree Cotton	country	tons	0.22	0.45	0.23
Bananas	country	stems	1,200	2,500	1,300
Cacao	country	tons	0.20	0.60	0.40
Coffee[a]	country	tons	0.60	1.20	0.60
Oranges	country	100's	500	1300	800
Grapes	country	tons	4.00	12.00	8.00
Temporary Crops					
Cotton[b]	country	tons	0.60	1.30	0.70
Peanuts	country	tons	0.90	1.80	0.90
Rice					
1	south[c]	tons	1.50	3.00	1.50
2	remainder	tons	1.20	2.40	1.20
Potatoes	country	tons	4.20	10.80	6.60
Sugar Cane					
1	four states[d]	tons	25.00	45.00	20.00
2	south[c]	tons	35.00	60.00	25.00
3	remainder	tons	30.00	50.00	20.00
Beans	country	tons	0.55	1.10	0.55
Tobacco					
1	south[c]	tons	0.60	1.50	0.90
2	remainder	tons	0.45	1.05	0.60
Mandioca	country	tons	10.00	20.00	10.00
Corn	country	tons	1.20	2.10	0.90
Wheat	country	tons	0.50	1.10	0.60
Cattle					
1	north and central-west[e]	head	0.50	1.00	0.50
2	Rio Grande do Sul	head	0.75	1.50	0.75
3	remainder	head	0.65	1.30	0.65

a   Cherries each containing two berries.

b   Bolls containing seeds.

c   São Paulo, Paraná, Santa Catarina, and Rio Grande do Sul.

d   Espírito Santo, Minas Gerais, Rio de Janeiro, and Guanabara.

e   Rondônia, Acre, Amapá Roraíma, Pará, Amazonas, Minas Gerais, Goiás, and the Distrito Federal.

TABLE 4

Calculation of the AYF for the Bragança Paulista Holding

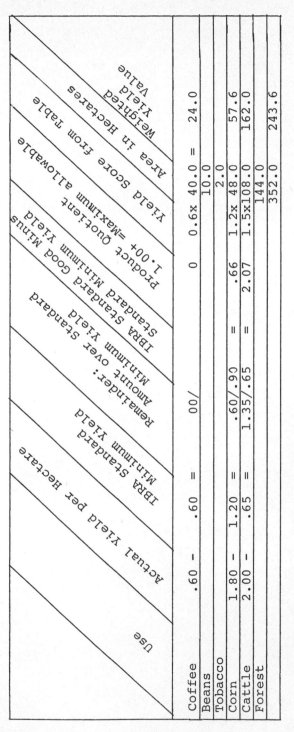

Use	Actual Yield per Hectare		IBRA Standard Minimum Yield		Remainder: Amount over Standard Minimum Yield	IBRA Standard Good Minus Standard Minimum Yield	Product Quotient 1.00+ = Maximum allowable	Yield Score from Table	Area in Hectares		Weighted Yield Value
Coffee	.60	-	.60	=	00/	0	0	0.6x	40.0	=	24.0
Beans									10.0		
Tobacco									2.0		
Corn	1.80	-	1.20	=	.60/	.90	= .66	1.2x	48.0	=	57.6
Cattle	2.00	-	.65	=	1.35/	.65	= 2.07	1.5x	108.0	=	162.0
Forest									144.0		
									352.0		243.6

243.6/352.0 = Agricultural Yields Factor of 0.6

TABLE 5

Translation of Product Quotients to Yield Scores

Product Quotients	Yield Score
negatives	0.5
0-0.15	0.6
0.16-0.25	0.7
0.26-0.35	0.8
0.36-0.45	0.9
0.46-0.55	1.0
0.56-0.65	1.1
0.66-0.75	1.2
0.76-0.85	1.3
0.86-1.00	1.4
above 1.00	1.5

a latifundio by use. A series of 1.5 yield scores
from production above IBRA standard good yields
will produce a 1.5 AYF--well above the disqualifying
limit. If the actual yield in one use is below the
IBRA standard minimum yield, another use can compensate, as corn and cattle almost compensate for
coffee on the Braganca holding.

IBRA clearly refuses to take seriously production figures in excess of the standard good
yield. In Table 3, note that the standard good
yield minus the standard minimum yield divided by
the difference between them (b-a/b-a) is always 1.0.
This is the highest allowable product quotient no
matter what it actually works out to be. For example, cattle production on the Bragança holding is
reported as 2.00 head per hectare, well above the
1.30 head IBRA standard good yield. But the actual
quotient of 2.00 is treated as 1.00+ and translates
to a yield score of 1.5 (Table 5). In this way
IBRA copes with declarations of excessive yields
whether these result from errors, ignorance, or
deliberate falsification.

From the foregoing, it is apparent that IBRA
feels its standard good yields to be well above
average, even approaching the upper limit of Brazilian agriculture's productive capacity. This is
verified by Table 6, which shows the IBRA good
yield for every use to be well above the 1960 Brazilian average. In addition, IBRA good yields are
larger than even U.S. average cotton and peanut
yields for 1961, and good yields for rice and to-
bacco in Brazil's south and for sugar cane in most
of the country are not far below those for the
United States in 1961. By any measure, however,
both the IBRA and the Brazil 1960 corn and wheat
yields per acre are pitifully low.

THE ECONOMIC YIELDS FACTOR

The Economic Yields Factor (EYF) is a measure
of the degree to which the actual annual gross income of a property approaches or exceeds its
potential annual gross income as established by
IBRA. Potential gross income is the number of
modulos on a property multiplied by 4 (the number
of working adults per modulo), by the federally set
monthly minimum regional salary, by 12 (number of
months in a year). The actual gross income of the

TABLE 6

Comparison of Yields:
IBRA Minimum and Good, Brazil, 1960, and United States, 1961

(All yields given in pounds per acre except where specified.)

Use	IBRA Minimum	IBRA Good	Brazil 1960	U.S. 1961
Tree Cotton	196	401		
Bananas	485 stems	790 stems	562 stems	
Cacao	178	535	308	
Coffee	535	1070	835	
Oranges	20242 units	52615 units	30154 units	
Grapes	3569	10707	6200	
Cotton[a]	535	1160	488	519
Peanuts	803	1606	1262	1220
Rice				
(1) south[b]	1338	2678	1605	3423
(2) remainder	1071	2142	1275	
Sugar Cane				
(1) four states[c]	22307	40153	14807	
(2) south[b]	31230	53538	32022	38200
(3) remainder	26761	62462	46294	
Beans	500	1000	601	1400
Tobacco				
(1) south[b]	535	1338	820	1755
(2) remainder	401	936	570	
Mandioca	8923	17846	11677	
Corn	1071	2141	1155	4650
	14 bu.	28 bu.	15 bu.	62 bu.
Wheat	446	1002	556	1965
	6 bu.	13 bu.	7 bu.	26 bu.

a Brazilian cotton includes seeds. U.S. cotton yield is a summation of fiber, linter, and seed yields.

b South: São Paulo, Parana, Santa Catarina, and Rio Grande do Sul.

c Four states: Espírito Santo, Minas Gerais, Rio de Janeiro, and Guanabara.

Brazil source: IBGE, Anuário Estatístico, 1961.

U.S. source: Statistical Abstract of the United States, 1963.

property as reported by the owner on his questionnaire is then divided by the potential. The resultant quotient is a measure of the degree to which
the potential is realized.

Although the range of this quotient is theoretically very great, IBRA sets practical limits of
0.3 and 2.5 (Table 7). This means that a property
gets no credit for an EYF if its actual income is
less than 30 per cent of its potential. At the
other end of the scale, a holding gets no additional
EYF credit for an actual income that exceeds 250 per
cent of its potential income. Using Table 7, IBRA
translates the quotient into the Economic Yields
Factor, which ranges from zero to five in units of
one. An EYF of zero (actual income less than 30
per cent of potential) disqualifies a property,
making it a latifundio by use.

TABLE 7

Translation of Income Quotient
into Economic Yields Factor

Income Quotient Actual over Potential	Economic Yields Factor	
less than 0.3	0	disqualifier
0.3 - 0.7	1	limit
0.8 - 1.2	2	
1.3 - 1.8	3	
1.9 - 2.4	4	
2.5 and over	5	

Calculation of the EYF, based on actual data
for a Bragança Paulista holding, is as follows:

17 modulos on the property
x4 adult workers supported by each modulo
68 adult workers supportable by the property

Cr$ 100,000 regional monthly minimum salary per
              adult
          x12 months
Cr$ 1,200,000
          x68 adults to be supported
Cr$86,600,000 potential annual gross income from
              holding

Cr$79,000,000 actual annual gross income reported
              by owner
              (proprietor + sharecropper + tenant
              incomes)

   Cr$79,000,000/Cr$81,600,000 = quotient of .97

   From Table 7   Economic Yields Factor = 2.

TWO NONDIFFERENTIATING COMPONENTS OF THE CEY

Even if a given property achieves acceptable
levels in its UF, AYF, and EYF, it may still have a
coefficient of Economic Yields that prevents its
classification as an empresa rural. The CEY is
based partially upon the AYF, the UF, and the EYF,
but also depends upon two other factors, the Investment Factor (IF), and the Bookkeeping Factor (BF).

The Investment Factor is a statement of the
degree to which a property is capitalized, and in a
sense is a partial measure of capital improvements
on a property by its total value (value of unimproved land + value of improvements). (See Table 8).
In the IBRA system, capital improvements include
buildings, implements, and equipment, perennial-
crop plantings, animals, and woodlots (whether natural or planted). Depending upon the magnitude of
the investment quotient, the property is assigned
an Investment Factor from Table 9, ranging from
zero to four in units of one.

If no improvements are reported by the owner,
IBRA sets their value at twice the value of the
unimproved land. This always produces an investment quotient of .67, since $2x/x+2x = .67$. (See
Table 10.) If an owner reports a land value less
than the minimum set by IBRA for the physiographic
zone in which his property is located (Cr$81,000
per hectare for Bragança Paulista), it is raised
to the minimum to determine the property's IF.

TABLE 8

```
              Calculation of the Investment Factor
           for  an Actual Bragança Paulista Property

Unimproved Land                                Cr$ 50,970,000
        272.2 hectares;
        value per hectare       Cr$   187,248
  Improvements
        Buildings               Cr$29,210,000
        Implements              Cr$ 2,500,000
        Equipment               Cr$ 6,700,000
        Perennial Crops         Cr$20,000,000
        Animals                 Cr$ 9,850,000
        Forest                  Cr$20,000,000
Total Value of Improvements                    Cr$ 89,210,000
Total Property Value                           Cr$140,180,000

Cr$89,210,000/Cr$140,180,000 = .63 investment quotient.
From Table 9, a .63 quotient = Investment Factor of 3.
```

TABLE 9

Translation of Investment Quotient into Investment Factor

Investment Quotient Improvements/Land + Improvements	Investment Factor
less than 0.20	0
0.21 - 0.40	1
0.41 - 0.60	2
0.61 - 0.80	3
more than 0.80	4

TABLE 10

```
     Calculation of the Investment Factor if No Land and
  Improvement Values Are Reported for the Bragança Holding

Unimproved Land                             Cr$22,048,200
     272.2 hectares    Cr$81,000 per hectare
Improvements                                Cr$44,096,400
     2x the value of the unimproved
Total Property Value                        Cr$66,144,600
Cr$44,096,400/Cr$66,144,600= .66 investment quotient.
From Table 9, a .66 quotient = Investment Factor of 3.
```

IBRA's credulity regarding the degree of investment has its limits. As indicated on Table 9,
the highest allowable investment quotient is 0.8.
This means that IBRA gives no credit to improvements valued at more than 80 per cent of the total
value of the property. Any amount above this is
simply assigned an IF of four. But improvements
must be at least 20 per cent of the value of a
property's land and improvements if it is to escape
an IF of zero.

The Investment Factor is not itself a disqual-
ifier of potential empresas rurais, but it may play
a role in determining whether a property is to be
disqualified on the basis of its AYF. The Agricultural Yields Factor of a holding for which no
basic uses are reported is calculated by multiplying the EYF, which ranges from zero to five, by the
IF, which has a zero to four range. This product,
ranging from zero to twenty, is then translated into the AYF, as shown in Table 11. Obviously, the
higher the IF and EYF, the higher the AYF, and if
the AYF is 0.6 or less, the property becomes a
latifundio by use.

TABLE 11

For a Property Not Reporting Basic Uses:
Determining Its AYF from Its Economic Yields Factor
and Its Investment Factor

Economic Yields Factor times Investment Factor	Agricultural Yields Factor	
1 and 2	0.5	
3 and 4	0.6	disqualifier
5 and 6	0.7	limit
8	0.8	
9	0.9	
10	1.0	
12	1.1	
14	1.2	
15	1.3	
16	1.4	
20	1.5	

The Bookkeeping Factor is much simpler in its derivation. If a propertyholder states that he keeps records of expenditures and receipts, he is awarded two points;if not, his BF is zero.

Final Derivation of the CEY

To derive the CEY, the EYF, the IF, and the BF are added together, and this total multiplied by the product of the AYF and UF. This product can be as low as zero:

EYF + IF + BF x (AYF x UF)

0 + 0 + 0 x (0.5 x 0) = 0

or it can be as high as 16.5:

EYF + IF + BF x (AYF x UF)

5 + 4 + 2 x (1.5 x1.0) = 11 x 1.5=16.5

But IBRA's upper allowable limit is 11. The resultant score is then subtracted from 15 and the difference divided by 10 to yield the CEY, which ranges from 0.4 to 1.5. The lower the score, the higher the degree to which the property has achieved IBRA's composite values with respect to: (1) the use of potentially productive land; (2) productivity; (3) income; (4) capital investment; (5) business-like operation (expressed in the keeping of records). A CEY of 1.3 or greater disqualifies a property from empresa rural status.

All five components are not equally strong in the derivation of the CEY. The EYF, IF, and BF are weak because they are only added. Thus a zero for any one or even two of these Factors still permits a positive result. But the AYF and UF are multiplied together. If either of these is a zero their product is zero, and when this is multiplied by the sum of the other three components the final product is zero. The resulting CEY would be 1.5, the worst possible, since (15-0)/10 = 1.5. IBRA clearly allows crop productivity (AYF) and the use of potentially productive land (UF) to exert the strongest influence on the CEY.

Zero or low values in these two components account for most of the 1.4 million Brazilian rural holdings with CEY's of 1.5 (Table 12). In addition to the 43 per cent at 1.5, another 34 per cent are at 1.3 and 1.4. Obviously, some of these properties are also eliminated from empresa rural status on the basis of their size, but even were they of

acceptable size, 78 per cent of the nation's properties could not meet the IBRA standards with respect to their Coefficients of Economic Yields.

TABLE 12

Number of Brazilian Rural Holdings at Each CEY Level		
CEY	Number of Properties	Per Cent of Total
0.4	15,360	.40
0.5	10,075	.30
0.6	21,536	.60
0.7	21,023	.60
0.8	39,618	1.10
0.9	66,782	1.90
1.0	73,891	2.10
1.1	207,851	6.10
1.2	282,000	8.40 disqualifier
1.3	478,308	14.20 limit
1.4	708,091	21.10
1.5	1,439,523	43.20
Total	3,364,063	100.00

The few remaining potential empresas rurais,
having emerged from the modulo and CEY gauntlets,
still have to pass a test of their social conditions before IBRA grants them final empresa rural
status.

CHAPTER **4** THE COEFFICIENT OF
SOCIAL CONDITIONS:
THE FIFTH SECOND-LEVEL
CRITERION

The Coefficient of Social Conditions (CSC)
has three components: the Administrative Factor
(AF), the Habitation and Sanitation Factor (HSF),
and the Education Factor (EF). (See Figure 5.)
The AF is designed to measure land-tenure conditions and levels of economic justice in the relationships between the landholder and his tenants
and/or sharecroppers. The derivation of the factor
demonstrates that in the new Brizilian agriculture
a higher value is to be placed on owner-operated
farms. Nevertheless, IBRA recognizes that tenancy
and sharecropping will be integral parts of the
rural scene for many years to come, and thus takes
steps to insure the proper distribution of rewards
to tenants and sharecroppers. The HSF and the EF,
on the other hand, are measures of the degree to
which a propertyowner fulfills his traditional role
as provider of basic housing and educational needs
for the people who live and work on his land.

THE ADMINISTRATIVE FACTOR

The Administrative Factor (AF) ranges from
zero to six and is a composite measure of:
1. The degree of participation of the owner
and his family in administering and working the
land and the conditions of wage laborers on the
property, which together result in the Owner-
Family-Laborer Score (OFLS);
2. The degree to which rewards to tenants and
sharecroppers meet standards defined in the Land
Statute, resulting in scores for the sharecropper
(SHS) and the tenant (TS).

FIGURE 5

Development of the Coefficient of Social Conditions

OPN OWNER PARTICIPATION NOTE. 0-3. Score based on whether owner administers property directly (yes = 1), possesses other remunerative activities (no = 1), and lives on the property (yes = 1).

FPN FAMILY PARTICIPATION NOTE. 0-1. Corporate control of property (no family responsibility) score = 1. With family control a zero is assessed only if fewer than half of the family group works the property.

WLN WAGE LABORER NOTE. 0-2. The more wage laborers the larger the number of five specified good labor practices owner must employ. If he employs 4 or 5 he gets a 2 regardless of the number of laborers.

OFLS OWNER-FAMILY-LABORER SCORE 0-6
0-6 times the area used by the family = af

CNs CONTRACT NOTE. 0-2.
No. of written contracts + No. of written & oral contracts for 3 years or more/
Number of sharecroppers

SNs SHARES NOTE. 0 or 2. Owner's actual share of produce must not exceed share to which he is legally entitled (50% in most cases).

SHS SHARECROPPER SCORE 0-4
0-4 times the area used by sharecroppers = as

CNt CONTRACT NOTE. 0-1.
No. of written contracts + No. of written & oral contracts for 3 years or more/
Number of tenants.

RNt RENT NOTE. 0 or 2.
Rent cannot exceed 15% of the total value of the land rented.
In very special cases where selected lands are rented for intensive
cultivation the owner may receive as much as 30%.

TS TENANT SCORE   0-3
0-3 times the area used by tenants = at

HABITATION AND SANITATION SCORE = 4. If there are fewer than six families or fewer than 26 persons on the property it receives a score of 4. There are no social responsibilities below these occupance levels.

OR

THE BEDROOM SCORE. 0-1. IBRA demands at least one bedroom for every five persons on the property.

A.

THE FLOOR/WALL SCORE. 0-1. IBRA demands that the number of clay walls plus the number of dirt floors not equal or exceed the total number of dwellings on the property.

B.

THE WATER SCORE. 0-1. IBRA demands that at least half the dwellings on the property be situated within 100 meters of a well, faucet or spring.

C.

THE LATRINE SCORE. 0-1. IBRA demands that there be at least one latrine for each 30 persons on the property.

D.

EDUCATION SCORE = 3. If there are fewer than six families or fewer than 26 persons or no children between the ages of 7 and 14 on the property the owner is absolved of an educational responsibility and scores 3.

OR

EAS EDUCATIONAL ATTENDANCE SCORE. 0-2. IBRA demands that at least half the number of children between 7 and 14 years of age attend school. If so, score = 0. Less than half = 1. None = 2.

ESS EDUCATIONAL SUPPORT SCORE. 0-1. IBRA demands that owner provide two or more of five specified school-related needs to score a zero. If he provides fewer than two he scores 1.

THE SOURCE OF THE DATA: THE GREAT LAND INVENTORY
3.5 million landholders or their proxies supplied information of questionnaires

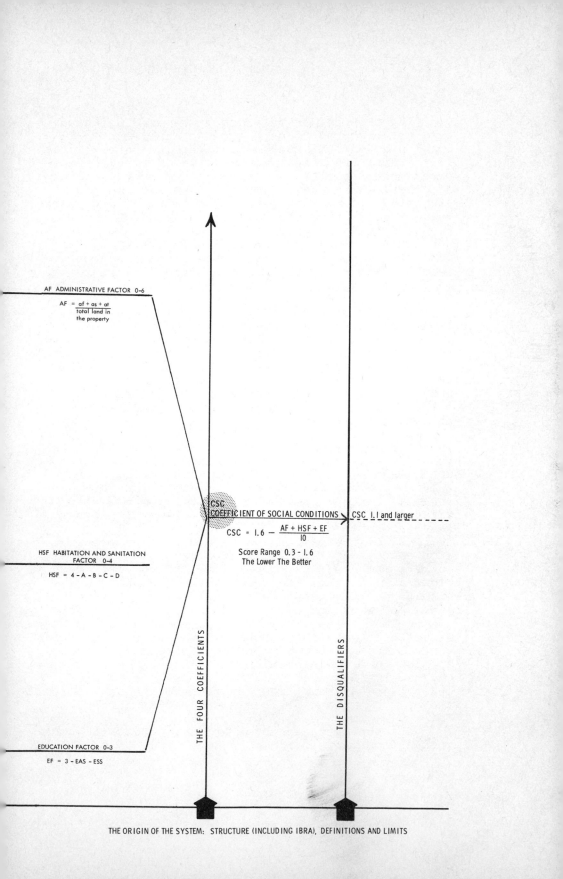

AF ADMINISTRATIVE FACTOR 0-6

AF = af + as + at
total land in
the property

CSC
COEFFICIENT OF SOCIAL CONDITIONS   CSC 1.1 and larger

$$CSC = 1.6 - \frac{AF + HSF + EF}{10}$$

Score Range 0.3 - 1.6
The Lower The Better

HSF HABITATION AND SANITATION
FACTOR 0-4

HSF = 4 – A – B – C – D

EDUCATION FACTOR 0-3

EF = 3 – EAS – ESS

THE FOUR COEFFICIENTS

THE DISQUALIFIERS

THE ORIGIN OF THE SYSTEM: STRUCTURE (INCLUDING IBRA), DEFINITIONS AND LIMITS

Owner-Family-Labor Score

The OFLS is derived from three measurements that are referred to as "Notes." The Owner Participation Note (OPN) ranges from zero to three (Table 13). To achieve the maximum value of three, the owner must directly administer his property, have no other remunerative activity, and live on his property. If he administers the holding, one point is subtracted from the maximum for each of the last two conditions on which he defaults. If he does not administer the property directly, his highest possible total for participation is one, and he receives this only if he has a hired administrator on the holding.

The Family Participation Note (FPN) assigned is either one or zero. The value of one is assigned to those properties whose owners are either corporations or partnerships, those whose proprietors have no able dependents of working age, and those on which one half or more of the dependents in condition to work actually do work on the land (Table 14). If fewer than half of these dependents work, the note is zero.

The third component of the OFLS, the Wage Labor Note (WLN), ranges from zero to two and is determined by the number of workers employed on a holding and the quality of labor relations as reflected in the number of positive responses to five questions (Table 15). If an owner employs no wage laborers, the five questions do not apply and he receives the maximum value of 2. If a proprietor employs at least one but fewer than twenty workers, he need answer only one of the five questions affirmatively to receive the maximum value; with no positive responses he receives a note of one. An owner who employs 20 to 100 laborers gets the maximum value of two only if he says yes to at least three questions. One or two positive answers gives him a note of one; no affirmative responses, a zero. A proprietor with more than 100 workers may receive a one only if he answers yes to at least two questions. He can recieve the maximum of two only by making at least four positive responses.

The sum of these three Notes is the OFLS which varies from zero to six.

Sharecropper Score

The sharecropper component of the AF may vary from zero to four. It is the sum of the Contract Note (CNs) and the Share Note (SNs).

The Contract Note is an evaluation of the contractual arrangements between sharecropper and owner. It is arrived at by first adding the number of written contracts and the number of contracts for terms of three years or more, then dividing this figure by the total number of sharecroppers on the property. The tens are rounded off so the final Note will be zero, one, or two. For example, if each of ten sharecroppers has a written contract for three years, then the owner's note will be two, because ten written plus ten for three years equals twenty, divided by ten sharecroppers. If no contract is written, but each is for a term of three years, then the note is one, because ten written divided by ten sharecroppers equals one. Oral contracts for less than three years are simply not recognized by IBRA.

The Shares Note is based on the percentage of sharecropper production received by the proprietor compared to the percentage to which he is legally entitled by Article 96 of the Land Statute. In exceptional cases, in zones of very extensive grazing, owners may legally share in up to 75 per cent of production. In all other areas and circumstances, the upper limit is 50 per cent. The specific share allowed by law depends upon the needs and capital items the owner supplies to the sharecropper. These items and the associated legal shares are listed in Table 16.

The proprietor indicates whether he provides any of the items listed in the first five categories. He receives ten points for each affirmative answer in categories one, two, and three, and twenty points if he answers yes in either four or five. IBRA recognizes that the items in categories four and five are mutually exclusive, that they pertain to different types of rural activities unlikely to be undertaken by a single sharecropper at the same time. The items in category six apply only to sharegrazing in extensively used zones of the country. Here, an owner is entitled to 75 per

TABLE 13

Owner Participation on Property

Owner Administers Property Directly	Has No Other Remunerative Activity	Lives on Property	3
		Does Not Live on Property	2
	Has Other Remunerative Activity	Lives on Property	2
		Does Not Live on Property	1
Does Not Administer Property Directly	Maintains Administrator on Property		1
	Does Not Maintain Administrator on Property		0

TABLE 14

Family Participation on Property

Owner is a Physical Person and Partner or a Legal Person			1
Physical Person is the Sole Owner	Does Not Have Family and Dependents on Land		1
	Has Family, Dependents on the Land	No One on Land Able to Work	1
		Some Able to Work	Half or More Work	1
			Fewer than Half Do	0

TABLE 15

Wage Labor on Property

| No. of Positive Responses to the Five Questions | Maximum Number of Wage Laborers | | |
	Fewer than 20	20-100	More than 100
0	1	0	0
1	2	1	0
2	2	1	1
3	2	2	1
4	2	2	2
5	2	2	2

THE FIVE QUESTIONS:

   Do you maintain a register of wage laborers?
   Do you maintain a stock of foods for wage laborers?
   Do you provide land for wage laborers to grow food?
   Do you forbid payment of wage laborers in other than money?
   Do you maintain receipts of payments to wage laborers?

cent of the return only if breed animals make up 25
per cent of the herd he supplies the sharegrazer
and if the sharegrazer gets half the milk produced
and receives a 5 per cent commission on each head
sold.

TABLE 16

Calculation of the Shares Note

Points		Items Supplied to Sharecropper by Owner
1.	10	cleared cropland or pasture
2.	10	housing
3.	10	basic farm construction (corrals, out-buildings, etc.)
and		
4.	20	agricultural machinery and implements, seeds, draught animals
or		
5.	20	livestock (if breed animals make up more than 50% of the herd)
	$\overline{50}$ —	50%, maximum share to which owner is entitled
or		
6.	75	In zones of very extensive grazing if: breed animals make up more than 25% of the herd and sharegrazer gets half the milk produced and sharegrazer receives a 5% commission per head sold.
	$\overline{75}$ —	75%, maximum share to which owner is entitled.

    The owner's legal percentage is then compared
with the percentage he actually receives from the
sharecropper or sharegrazer. If the actual percentage is less than or equal to the legal share
determined by the process above, the owner receives
an SNs of 2; otherwise his Note is zero.

    The Contract Note (CNs) and the Shares Note
(SNs) are then added to yield the SHS, the sharecropper component of the Administrative Factor (AF).

Significantly, the maximum sharecropper score is
four, while that for the owner-family-laborer component is six. It is clear that sharecropping does
not stand as high in Brazilian agrarian-reform
values as family farm operation. As should be noted later, any property on which sharecropping is
practiced, even on part of the land, cannot achieve
the best possible score on the Coefficient of Social
Conditions.

Tenant Score

The method for calculating the tenant component
of the AF is similar to that used for the sharecropper score. It involves a quantification of contractual arrangements to yield the Contract Note
(CNt) and compares tenant rent payments with levels
fixed by IBRA to produce the Rent Note (RNt). There
is, however, one significant difference. The Contract Note for tenants (CNt) is obviously meant to
parallel that for sharecroppers (CNs). It is calculated in exactly the same way and so might be expected to have a range of zero to two. Nevertheless,
the highest value that can be awarded for this note
is one. The Rent Note (RNt) parallels the Share
Note (SNs) and is calculated in the following manner:
The rent received by the owner for the parcel is divided by the parcel's total value (land plus improvements)and the quotient is multiplied by 100. This
figure, which is the percentage of the rented land's
value annually returned to the owner, is then compared with the actual rent received by the owner for
the parcel. If he receives 15 per cent or less his
note is two; if more than 15 per cent, his note is
zero. In very special cases, where selected lands
are rented for intensive cultivation, the owner may
receive up to 30 per cent of the land value in rent.
The absence of any of the information necessary to
establish this Note yields the owner a zero.

Since the maximum value of the CNt is one and
of the RNt two, the maximum value of the Tenant
Score is three. Since the maximum sharecropper
score is four, properties with tenants are likely to
have lower AF's than those with sharecroppers. One
administrator in IBRA justifies this situation by
stating that sharecroppers are deemed likely to be
more productive than tenants within the Brazilian
agricultural structure.

Final Derivation of the Administrative Factor

The Owner-Family-Laborer Score (OFLS), Share-cropper Score (SHS), and Tenant Score (TS) are now weighted by the area worked under each arrangement by multiplying each of the scores by the area under its kind of control. The sum of these products is divided by the total area of the property to yield the Administrative Factor (AF). For example:

Tenure Arrangement   Hectares   Maximum
                                Score

Owner-Family-Laborer   100   x   6 = 600
Sharecropper   100   x   4 = 400
Tenants   100   x   3 = 300
                                     1,300/300=4.3

        Administrative Factor = 4

Note that regardless of the actual conditions of tenants or sharecroppers, any property with such tenure arrangements is prevented from attaining the maximum AF of six. The greater the percentage of the holding in tenancy and/or sharecropping, the less its maximum potential AF. This fact reflects the premium being placed on owner-family operations in Brazilian agriculture.

THE HABITATION AND SANITATION FACTOR
AND THE EDUCATION FACTOR

To determine the Habitation and Sanitation Factor (HSF) and the Education Factor (EF), rural properties are divided into two groups according to the level of responsibility IBRA expects the owners to assume.

The first group is made up of those properties whose owner is felt to have no responsibilities for the HSF and EF. Into this group fall those properties on which live fewer than six families and fewer than twenty-six persons and no children between the ages of seven and fourteen. A holding in this category is automatically assigned an HSF of four and an EF of three. These perfect scores follow because of the small number of dependent people involved and the absence of school-age children reduce the owner's level of responsibility for providing such needs.

The owners of properties on which live more than five families or more than twenty-five persons or at least one child between seven and fourteen years of age are scored on their responses to the following questions:

1. Is there at least one bedroom for every five persons on the property? Yes = 1, No = 0.

2. Is the number of clay walls + the number of dirt floors equal to or less than one half the total number of dwellings on the property? Yes = 1, No = 0. (For example, of fifty dwellings on a given property any combination of clay walls and dirt floors must total twenty-five or less.)

3. Are at least half the dwellings situated within 100 meters of a well, faucet, or spring? Yes = 1, No = 0.

4. Is there at least one latrine for each thirty persons on the property? Yes = 1, No = 0.

5. How many children between the ages of seven and fourteen attend school? Half or more = 2, Fewer than half = 1, None = 0.

6. Does the owner supply two or more of the following school-related needs? Yes = 1, No = 0.
   a. school building
   b. teacher
   c. transportation to classes
   d. clothes or shoes to pupils
   e. books and materials

The scores on the first four questions are added to yield the HSF. The EF is calculated by adding the scores on the final two questions. The maximum value for the HSF is four, and for the EF three.

THE COEFFICIENT OF SOCIAL CONDITIONS

Once the AF (0-6), the HSF (0-4), and the EF (0-3) are established, they are added and this total divided by 10. This quotient is then subtracted from 1.6, and the result is the Coefficient of Social Conditions (CSC), ranging from 0.3 to 1.6. This Coefficient stands in inverse relationship to the degree to which the property-holder has achieved IBRA standards; the lower the CSC the better. A Coefficient greater than 1.0 is sufficient to disqualify a holding from empresa rural status.

A reader who has waded through the derivation of the CSC is probably much less in a frame of mind to consider a detailed critique of its internal logic than to level a broadside at the Coefficient's inordinately complex and unwieldy structure. This complexity, besides compounding inaccuracies, guesses, and undoubtedly some falsehoods, obscures the relationship between an owner's defaulting on one or a series of IBRA requirements and the ensuing penalty. At the end of an exhausting calculation, an owner may find his property above 1.0 and have no idea why. It is apparent that IBRA assigns priorities to tenure, living, and educational conditions in that order, but their actual effect on the CSC is not readily identifiable. Delineation of some sub-CSC disqualifiers, as was done for the CEY, would help to clarify the default-penalty association. The small amount of CSC data IBRA has cared to make public, which, incidentally, does not even include the number of spatial distribution of properties disqualified by the Coefficient, is traceable in part to the lack of significant sub-CSC results.

The Coefficient serves primarily to organize information gathered from the Land Inventory questionnaire and the sharecropper and tenant annexes. What information is available provides a limited picture of rural labor and land tenure conditions, but one that is credible. The number of rural laborers, sharecroppers, and tenants (Table 17) does at first seem small, but there is reason to believe that the total is fairly accurate and well represents the rural half of the Brazilian population. The 6.3 million persons who have entered into some kind of contract with landowners are virtually all male and most are heads of families. That each supports himself and four other persons (five in all) is hardly a radical estimate. Given these assumptions, the 6.3 million workers would support a total of 31.5 million rural people, or just under half the 75 million Brazilians estimated for 1966. Even if the support figure is reduced, thereby reducing the rural total, this loss could easily be compensated for by the untold numbers of migratory agriculturalists and squatters in the backlands who neither owned land nor made any kind of contract with a landowner, and who, as a consequence, were untouched by the Land Inventory.

TABLE 17

Number and Density of Wage Laborers, Sharecroppers, and Tenants in Brazil, 1966

	Wage Laborers		Share-croppers	Tenants	Brazil Total
	permanent	peak			
No. of Persons	1,550,692	5,328,855	773,799	230,497	–
No. of Properties	750,695 22.3%		318,283 9.5%	111,741 3.3%	3,364,063 100.0%
No. of Hectares	–	–	9,763,500 7.0%	10,270,300 7.5%	137,759,000 100.0%
Hectares per sharecropper or tenant	–	–	12.6	44.6	–
Wage laborers, sharecroppers, tenants per property	2.0	7.2	2.4	2.0	–

Source: IBRA Land Inventory questionnaires, 1965-1967.

On the basis of sheer numbers, wage laborers
dominate the Brazilian rural scene. Three-quarters
of a million properties (22 per cent of the total)
supply permanent work for 1.5 million laborers and
employ a total of 5.3 million during periods of
heavy demand. This averages out to permanent employment for 2.0 laborers per property and peak-
period employment for 7.2 workers.

National wage-labor figures vary sharply from
one part of Brazil to another. Paraná and São Paulo
are the prime users of both permanent and temporary
wage labor (Table 18), due to the large labor demands of coffee crops. States in the east and the
northeast have the greatest fluctuations from a very
low permanent-wage labor base. Peak employment in
Minas Gerais, for example, is 6.6 times the permanent base, and in Piauí, 5.3 times.

Twelve per cent of Brazil's properties have
sharecroppers or tenants, and together they work 14
per cent of the total land area in the country's
rural holdings (Table 17). Since the sharecropper
density per property (2.4) is higher than the tenant
density (2.0), sharecropping is clearly the more
popular tenure arrangement with landowners. Nevertheless, in the aggregate, owners contract a bit
more land with tenants than with sharecroppers, and
since sharecroppers outnumber tenants by more than
three to one, each sharecropper is allocated only
12.6 hectares, compared to 44.6 hectares per tenant.

Sharecropper and tenant densities per property
vary widely from place to place in Brazil (Table 19).
Sharecropper densities are well above the national
mean in the Amazon-basin states of Acre and Rondônia,
the almost-feudal northeastern states of Sergipe and
Alagoas, and the more recently opened lands of
the Maranhão basin. The European family farm tra-
dition in the southern states of Santa Catarina and
Rio Grand do Sul keeps sharecropper densities low.
Tenant densities tend to be high in the north and
northeast. In Amazonas, Maranhão, Rio Grande do
Norte, Perambuco, and Bahia, and in the eastern
state of Guanabara as well, not only are tenant
densities much higher than the Brazilian mean, but
contrary to the national pattern they are also
higher than the sharecropper densities.

TABLE 18

Distribution by Political Unit of Permanent and
Maximum Wage Laborer Densities by Property

Political Unit	Wage Laborers per Property Permanent	Maximum	Maximum Exceeds Permanent By:
Paraná	4.6	12.0	
São Paulo	4.3	10.1	
Alagoas	2.9	7.9	
Mato Grosso	2.8	5.9	
Pernambuco	2.7	7.5	
Pará	2.4	6.9	
Amapá	2.4	6.0	
Amazonas	2.4	6.0	
Rio de Janeiro	2.4	5.2	
Rio Grande do Sul	2.2 --mean	4.9	
Ceará	1.8	6.7	
Acre	1.8	5.4	
Santa Catarina	1.8	4.1	
Maranhão	1.7	7.5	4.4x
Rondônia	1.7	5.4	
Paraíba	1.7	5.6	
Roraima	1.6	2.7	
Rio Grande do Norte	1.5	6.0	4.0x
Guanabara	1.5	3.2	
Minas Gerais	1.4	9.0	6.6x
Goiás	1.4	6.4	4.5x
Bahia	1.4	4.9	
Piauí	1.3	7.0	5.3x
Espírito Santo	1.3	5.4	4.1x
Sergipe	.9	4.6	5.1x
Distrito Federal	.6	3.1	5.1x
Brazilian Mean	2.0	7.2	3.6x

Source: IBRA Land Inventory questionnaires, 1965-1967.

TABLE 19

Distribution by Political Unit of Sharecropper and Tenant Densities by Property

Political Unit	Sharecroppers Per Property	Tenants Per Property
Acre	28.5	2.2
Rondônia	12.1	4.8
Sergipe	8.0	4.5
Maranhão	7.5	14.7
Alagoas	6.0	3.9
Ceará	4.8	2.5
Amazonas	3.6	3.7
Pernambuco	3.2	4.3
Piauí	3.1	2.7
Paraíba	2.9	7.5
Distrito Federal	2.8	-
Rio de Janeiro	2.8	1.8
Minas Gerais	2.7	1.3
Rio Grande do Norte	2.7	3.8
Goiás	2.5	2.1
Roraima	2.5	-
São Paulo	2.4 --mean	1.9
Espírito Santo	2.4	1.2
Bahia	2.2	2.7
Paraná	2.2	1.9
Mato Grosso	2.2	2.0
Pará	2.0	1.8
Guanabara	1.6	2.9
Santa Catarina	1.4	1.3
Rio Grande do Sul	1.3	1.2
Amapá	1.0	1.0

Brazilian Mean   2.4   2.0

Source: IBRA Land Inventory questionnaires, 1965-1967.

The number of hectares per sharecropper and per tenant (Table 20) tends to be above the national mean for each type of tenure in the larger, more sparsely populated states of the Amazon basin and the central-west, and below the mean in the smaller, more densely settled states of the east and north-east. A few states deviate sharply from the national averages. Ceará, Piauí, Goiás, and São Paulo are above the national mean in hectares per sharecropper, but well below in tenant hectarage.

The limited available CSC data and the flabby structure of the Coefficient suggest that it holds lower IBRA priority than does the CEY. Economic (agricultural)reform seems to take precedence over socio-economic (agrarian) reform. But urban migration has become a veritable flood and far too much existing capital is not going into rural development or incomes. A restructured and rigorously imple-mented CSC could well be instrumental in altering these conditions. Strict enforcement of many CSC provisions would seem to be imperative for keeping potentially productive people on the land and im-proving distribution of existing and future income.

PROPERTY CLASSIFICATIONS

As a result of the application of the system of property classification described in this and the two preceding chapters, four classes of property can be defined in quantitative terms. An empresa rural, the only type considered desirable by the Land Statute, can be described as a rural holding between one and 600 modulos in size, but not encompassing an acreage more than 600 times the zonal average, and meeting the following criteria:
1. UF (Utilization Factor) greater than 0.5, meaning that 50 per cent or more of the potentially productive land is used
2. AYF (Agricultural Yields Factor) greater than 0.6
3. EYF (Economic Yields Factor) of one or above, which according to an IBRA scale means that actual gross income is at least 30 per cent of po-tential gross income
4. CEY (Coefficient of Economic Yields) less than 1.3 (together three and four signify that methods of production on the property result in out-puts consistent with predetermined standards)

TABLE 20

Distribution by Political Unit of Hectares
per Sharecropper and Tenant

Political Unit	Hectares Per Sharecropper	Hectares Per Tenant
Acre	565.0	2080.0
Amazonas	471.0	160.0
Roraima	462.0	--
Pará	109.0	190.0
Amapá	50.0	66.0
Rondônia	47.0	4100.0
Mato Grosso	30.0	117.0
Goiás	23.0	39.0
Rio Grande do Sul	16.6	123.0
Ceará	16.5	26.0
Piauí	15.7	27.0
São Paulo	13.0	33.3
Paraíba	12.5	6.0
Rio Grande do Norte	12.2	19.5
Paraná	12.0	18.1
Santa Catarina	10.0	19.3
Espírito Santo	9.0	44.0
Pernambuco	8.8	14.4
Bahia	8.3	9.0
Maranhão	8.2	12.6
Minas Gerais	7.2	48.5
Distrito Federal	7.1	--
Alagoas	3.1	9.5
Sergipe	3.1	12.0
Guanabara	3.0	5.0
Rio de Janeiro	2.7	35.2

| Brazilian Mean | 12.6 | 44.6 |

Source: IBRA Land Inventory questionnaires, 1965-1967.

5. CSC (Coefficient of Social Conditions) less
than 1.1, indicating that the property meets the new
Brazilian standards of rural socio-economic justice.

All other holdings are classified either minifundios
(less than one modulo in size),latifundios by size
(larger than 600 modulos), or latifundios by use
(one to 600 modulos in size but not meeting all of
the second-level standards, i.e., UF, AYF, EYF, CEY,
and CSC).

A graphic presentation of IBRA's view of Brazilian agricultural reality as defined by this
system of classification is shown in Figure 6.
There is no attempt in this diagram to represent the
actual percentages of areas falling into the various
categories, nor to show their locations relative to
one another. Empresas rurais occupy the central
portion of the diagram because IBRA focuses on them
as the desirable units and because this facilitates
comparison with the other types of property units.

Latifundios by size, shown in white on the
diagram, either exceed 600 times the average size
property for a given zone or exceed 600 modulos. A
holding larger than 72,000 hectares must exceed the
600 modulo limit, since the largest standard modulo
is 120 hectares (forestry in the "D" zone class).

Each latifundio by use is given a symbol show-
ing the reason for its classification. The symbol
CSC indicates that the property in question has been
classified latifundio because its Coefficient of
Social Conditions exceeds 1.0. In a like manner,
the one having a Utilization Factor less than 0.5,
the one having an Agricultural Yield Factor less
than 0.7, and the one having a Coefficient of Economic Yield greater than 1.2 are shown by the
symbols UF, AYF, and CEY.

The minifundios are all less than 1 modulo in
size.

Some comments on the diagram should help to
clarify the IBRA system. Note that a few of the
empresas rurais are larger than any of the latifundios by use. Note also that some of the empresas
rurais are smaller than some of the minifundios, and
that at least one minifundio is larger than any of
the latifundios by use. These seeming incongruities
are a function of the application of the modulo
concept. Sheer size is not of prime import. Internal
organization and allocation of resources are the
critical factors in this system of classification.

FIGURE 6

Hypothetical Diagram of IBRA
Rural Property Classification

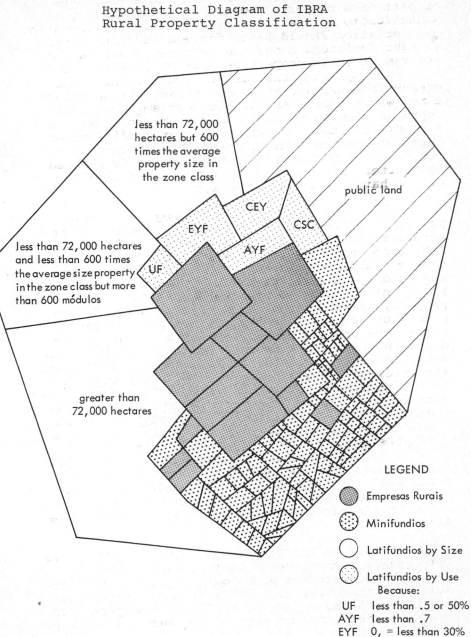

less than 72,000
hectares but 600
times the average
property size in
the zone class

public land

CEY

EYF

CSC

AYF

less than 72,000 hectares
and less than 600 times
the average size property
in the zone class but more
than 600 módulos

UF

greater than
72,000 hectares

LEGEND

Empresas Rurais

Minifundios

Latifundios by Size

Latifundios by Use
Because:

UF   less than .5 or 50%
AYF   less than .7
EYF   0, = less than 30%
CEY   greater than 1.2
CSC   greater than 1.0

PENALIZING THE UNACCEPTABLE

The Statute gives IBRA power to expropriate all or part of a property declared a latifundio by size, a latifundio by use, or a minifundio. The threat of expropriation should be sufficient to force owners to make decisions about the internal organization and use of their properties that will bring them into the empresa rural class. The only holdings exempt from expropriation are those outside priority zones whose owners are already implementing IBRA-approved plans directed toward a change in status in a specified time. Owners who alter conditions on their properties without prior IBRA sanction may petition for a change of status, which is granted only after IBRA confirms that the internal alterations have in fact taken place.

Insofar as the Statute is concerned, expropriation and abridgment of property rights are instruments for the placing of capable decision-makers on units of land of acceptable size. In the case of full expropriation, one decision-maker is replaced by another, presumably one better able to bring the property to acceptable status. Or, if the property is subdivided, one decision-maker is replaced by several. In the case of partial expropriation, the present owner's property is simply reduced in size by making room for a second decision-maker on a newly created acceptable-size land unit. The owner may, however, request full expropriation if his remaining cultivable area is less than 50 per cent of the original and partial expropriation reduces the rump to less than three modulos. He may also demand full expropriation if removal of a part does substantial economic damage to the rump, such as leaving it with a lower value than the expropriated section. In regions of minifundios, if an owner sells, he must do so to the owner of a contiguous property. Properties so conjoined are thus moved in the direction of or even up to acceptable size.

Title II of the Statute and Article 147 of the 1946 Federal Constitution (not brought into play until the Statute was promulgated) protect both the owner and the government in the expropriation process. In fixing a just price for the property, IBRA must take into account both the unimproved value of

the land, declared by the owner for the Rural Land
Tax, and the value of improvements, and then apply
any monetary correction called for by specific legislation in effect at the time. It also must take
into account the owner's possible overestimate or
falsification of these values. To take possession
of goods (other than unimproved land), IBRA is ob-
ligated to put up no more than the value the owner
(if he is a physical person) declares in his last
declaration of rural income, or the present market
value of the goods if the owner is a corporate person. Upon transfer of the goods, the owner is guaranteed 80 per cent of the amount put up by IBRA
(when he gets the other 20 per cent is not specified). Every decision fixing the price of a property above that determined by IBRA must be reviewed
by the Federal Appeals Court. Property expropriated
for specific cause is not subject to repossession
once in the public domain, and any court proceedings
against the expropriating power can be resolved only
in terms of losses and damages and not in return of
the property.

REDISTRIBUTION

     At the other end of the expropriation process
lies the redistribution of properties. Not all are
destined to become single-family farms, although
making land available to landless families and ex-
panding the properties of those whose holdings are
too small are prime reasons for redistribution. In
addition, however, the Statute makes expropriated
lands available to newly formed cooperatives dedi-
cated to farming, grazing, or agro-industrial activities. Lands are also to be made available to
federal, state, and local governments for reforesta-
tion and for agricultural research and experiment
stations.

     Lands are to be sold to prospective owners de-
pending upon the age (21), sanity, and good back-
ground (or rehabilitation) of these owners, in the
following order of preference:
     1. The former owner of the expropriated prop-
erty if he himself or a member of his family lives
on and works the holding
     2. Those who work the property as squatters,
wage workers, sharecroppers, or renters
     3. Farmers whose holdings are less than a
modulo in size

4. Those whose properties are too small to
sustain themselves and their families
5. Those who come under existing legislation
or who have special skills or competence to farm.

The heads of large families take precedence in each
group. New owners may borrow from the government an
amount equivalent to the annual minimum salary of
the region, to be repaid over 20 years at 6 per
cent.

Some persons are specifically barred from being
beneficiaries of expropriated lands. With the exception of those noted in the Statute, only persons
without land may acquire it. No one exercising a
public function or holding a position in a state or
federal authority can receive expropriated land.
Neither can a person in a quasi-government agency or
someone invested with quasi-fiscal powers.

Although the Federal Constitution of 1946 gives
the President of the Republic power to decree agrarian reform, a major and long-time deterrent to his
so doing was the fact that compensation for expropriated land had to be in cash, not bonds. Since
there were no laws for providing such funds, expropriation was out of the question, even on a limited
scale. The Statute, however, covers all these problems. It provides for sources of funds and brings
the weight of agrarian reform to bear on limited
areas of the country.

PRIORITY AREAS

The Statute requires that IBRA delimit areas
whose problems are acute and can best be treated by
a concentrated dose of reform embodied in regional
plans. Each of these priority areas is under the
aegis of a Delegacia Regional, or regional agency, of
IBRA (generally referred to as IBRAR), which is
instructed to make lavish use of the expropriation
weapon. The Delegacia fixes regional priorities,
determines the extent and location of expropriatable
areas, lays plans for needed development, and estimates the costs of all these works.

To date, five priority areas have been delimited (Figure 7). Among the three set up in 1965
is one in the northeast covering the eastern half of

FIGURE 7

Priority Areas Delimited by IBRA

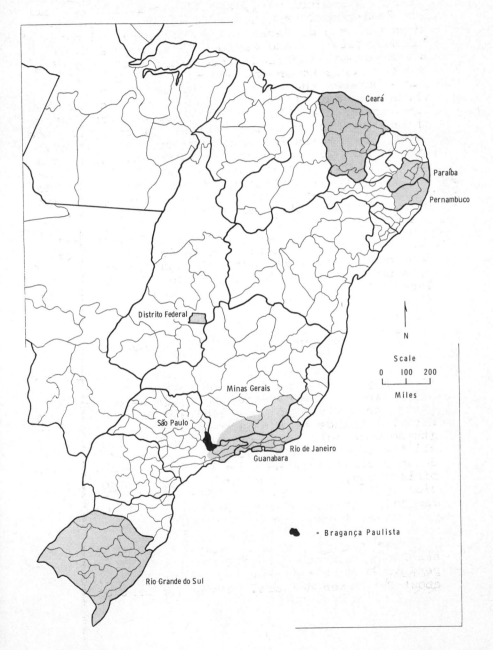

the state of Paraíba and the eastern third of Pernambuco. It includes the semi-arid, scrub-covered,
hilly interiors of these states (and thus the eroded
agave plantations of Paraíba) as well as their humid
litorals. The latter zones suffer from heavy rural
population pressure, latifundistas, low labor and
cane land productivity, and little available land
for food crops. Another area covers all of the
states of Rio de Janeiro and Guanabara and parts of
Minas Gerais and São Paulo. It incorporates
Brazil's most important interurban food-producing
region, focusing on the worn-out Paraíba Valley
lands between the country's two largest cities. The
third area established in 1965 is the Distrito Federal around Brasília, which is supposed to supply
the new capital with food crops. It comprises the
level but sterile Pratinha surface, recently given
over solely to cattle grazing, but now threatened
with wild and erratic rural nonfarm land-use expansion. In 1966, the entire state of Rio Grande do
Sul was declared a priority zone. The awful degree
of minifundioization among Brazil's pride and joy,
the German-, Italian-, and Polish-Brazilian farmers
on the northern plateau, and the latifundioization
on the rolling southern grasslands (campos) threaten
both output and rural economic and social health in
this potentially stable and productive state. Still
later, the dry northeastern state of Ceará became
IBRA's fifth priority area.

PAYING FOR AGRARIAN REFORM

     It takes money to plan and execute changes and
to expropriate. The Statute provides for this need
by setting up the National Agrarian Reform Fund.
Among the sources of this fund are fees paid to IBRA
for such things as the Land Inventory questionnaire
(these were sold and a processing fee also charged),
all the resources guaranteed by law to SUPRA (a now-
defunct agrarian agency set up by the previous ad-
ministration), resources received from agencies
closely linked to IBRA, and money from a special
federal improvement tax. But above all, IBRA is
guaranteed 3 per cent of federal tax receipts.

     The proposed federal budget for 1967 (Tables 21
and 22) envisioned a balancing of receipts with expenditures at 6 trillion 596 billion cruzeiros, or
about 2 billion dollars. Three per cent of this

amounts to 200 billion cruzeiros (62 million dollars).[1] Neither the agency nor the subject category
in Tables 21 and 22 shows 3 per cent of this budget
specified for IBRA. The 3 per cent may be included
in the Ministry of Agriculture's 3.3 per cent or in
Agriculture/Grazing's 6.1 per cent. In any event,
money for agrarian reform clearly has only a moder-
ate priority in this budget.

     According to IBRA, the 3.4 million properties
in Brazil whose questionnaires have been processed
have a total value (unimproved land + improvements)
of 25 trillion 156 billion cruzeiros. Although
fewer than 10 per cent of these properties are empresas rurais, not subject to expropriation, they
probably make up 20 per cent of the total value of Brazilian rural property. This leaves 20 trillion
cruzeiros of expropriatable property, a figure three
times the entire proposed federal budget for 1967.
At this rate (if no other factors changed), it would
take 100 years to redistribute Brazil's expropriable
lands. (Of course, money from the sale of expropriated properties would become available to help speed
this.) Thus the importance of the priority-area concept can be seen. Rio Grande do Sul's lands and
improvements are valued at 4 trillion 106 billion
cruzeiros, probably 3.3 trillion of which are expropriatable. Applying 200 billion cruzeiros per year
to the job, it would take 17 years to redistribute
all these properties. Although this certainly could
be considered a "very deliberate speed," it can be
accelerated (assuming land value increments and in-
flation to be circumscribed) as federal receipts
increase, as payments for redistributed land flow
back into the IBRA coffers, and as IBRA concentrates
on even more limited segments of these priority
zones. And the prospect for rural change need not
be so gloomy if the threat of expropriation and
abridgment serves to force changes on properties
without the replacement of owners.

     In summary, the Brazilian rural property clas-
sification system is aimed at identifying holdings
that for one reason or another are deemed undesirable in the light of national values and goals.
Owners of these properties are threatened with expropriation and other abridgments of property
rights. These threats, it is hoped, will encourage
or force latifundistas and minifundistas to make
decisions about the internal organization of their
properties and the uses to which they are put that

TABLE 21

Proposed Brazilian Federal Budget for 1967,
by Agency

	Amount in Old Cruzeiros	Per Cent
Total Proposed Budget	6 596 617 956 000	100.0
Executive Branch		
Ministry of Finance	1 695 625 547 000	25.7
Ministry of Transport	1 133 248 582 000	17.2
Ministry of War	643 684 436 000	9.8
Ministry of Education	616 674 682 000	9.4
Ministry of the Air Force	419 674 504 000	6.4
Ministry of Regional Organizations	369 941 519 000	5.6
Ministry of the Navy	353 673 600 000	5.4
Ministry of Mines and Energy	256 568 436 000	3.9
Ministry of Health	222 650 509 000	3.4
Ministry of Agriculture	221 469 816 000	3.3
Presidency of the Republic	161 097 509 000	2.4
Ministry of Justice	139 950 808 000	2.1
Ministry of Foreign Relations	100 204 915 000	1.6
Ministry of Labor	75 543 770 000	1.1
Ministry of Commerce and Industry	14 901 072 000	.2
Armed Forces Chiefs of Staff	13 072 000 000	.2
Legislative Branch		
Chamber of Deputies	53 060 000 000	.8
Senate	31 914 356 000	.5
Budget Bureau	7 918 303 000	negl.
National Economic Council	1 343 592 000	negl.
Judicial Branch		
Supreme Court	3 955 000 000	negl.
Labor Court	28 492 000 000	.4
Electoral Court	26 513 000 000	.4
Federal Court	5 500 000 000	negl.

Source: "O Congresso Nacional recebe proposta orcamentária para 67,"
Correio Brasiliense (August 2, 1966), p. 3.

TABLE 22

Proposed Brazilian Federal Budget for 1967,
by Category

Category	Amount in Old Cruzeiros	Per Cent
Total By Category	5 461 912 649 000	100.0
National Defense	1 125 149 422 000	20.4
Grants to states, federal district, and municípios	807 646 198 000	14.6
Transportation	770 727 932 000	14.1
Federal Debts	617 458 802 000	13.0
Social Security	593 471 714 000	10.7
Agriculture/Grazing	336 650 704 000	6.1
Mines and Energy	316 015 759 000	5.6
Health	232 329 136 000	4.2
Sanitation	153 727 953 000	2.8
Industry and Commerce	113 858 200 000	2.0
Internal Security	105 995 439 000	1.9
Foreign Policy	92 953 355 000	1.6
Housing and Public Service	66 482 525 000	1.2
Dam Building (in dry northeast)	59 992 536 000	1.0
Natural Resources	28 825 936 000	.5
Colonization and Settlement	20 627 038 000	.3

Source: "O Congresso Nacional recebe proposta orcamentária
para 67," Correio Brasiliense (August 2, 1966), p. 3.

will allow them to be classified as empresa rural,
the type of holding that IBRA considers essential to
the achievement of basic Brazilian economic and
social goals:
    1. Provision of more and cheaper agricultural
commodities
    2. Higher and more widely distributed rural
incomes
    3. Improved social conditions in rural areas
    4. A shift toward closer owner participation
in the productive process.

Each of these goals is in turn related to the broader objectives of stimulating expansion in the industrial sector of the economy by making available
cheap raw materials and wage goods and by relieving
or eliminating economic want and social tensions in
the countryside.

    In addition, all properties, even the empresas
rurais, are subject to taxation whose level depends
upon the degree to which they meet IBRA's social and
economic standards. Thus decision-making can be
affected through the whole spectrum of Brazil's
agrarian structure. The following chapter explores
the structure and significance of the new land tax
system.

NOTE

    1. The 1967 conversion rate was 3,200
cruzeiros per U.S. dollar.

CHAPTER **5** DIFFERENTIAL LAND
TAXATION

The system of property classification described
in the preceding three chapters gives IBRA a tool
for guiding or forcing decisions on the part of
landholders. The threat of expropriation or re-
strictions on property transfer or subdivision create incentives for landholders with unfavorable
classifications to change the internal organization
of their properties. As a result, more and more
land can be brought under economic and social
systems that are more nearly in line with Brazilian
ideals. Nevertheless, the criteria used in classification leave wide margins between what is acceptable and what is ideal. Many properties may lie
within acceptable bounds, but still be far below
their potential. Further, expropriation and other
direct abridgments of property rights are expensive
and fraught with political dangers, and because of
limited resources, direct action of this type may be
long delayed in parts of the country.

Differential land taxation is designed to bring
about change that is voluntary, less expensive, and
more immediate than expropriation, and at the same
time provide an incentive for improvements even on
empresas rurais. The tax is also designed, of
course, to raise revenues, and is computed as defined in the Statute and supplemental decrees.

THE LAND TAX

The land tax is made up of a constant (.002)
and five variables--the unimproved value and four
coefficients. Two of the coefficients, for Economic
Yields and for Social Conditions, have been already
discussed. To these are added the Coefficient of
Location and the Coefficient of Dimension.[1] Stated
simply, the land tax = .002 x the unimproved value

of the land x the Coefficient of Dimension x the
Coefficient of Location x the Coefficient of Economic Yields x the Coefficient of Social Conditions.

The coefficients have different but specified
ranges. The Coefficient of Dimension (CD) has the
widest absolute range, 1.0-4.5, while the Coefficient of Location (CL) has the narrowest, 1.0-1.6.
The CSC varies from 0.3 to 1.6, and the CEY from
0.4 to 1.5. Justification for these specific ranges
and their varying weights is nowhere provided in the
Land Statute or subsequent decree. Nor is their
differential impact clear. At first glance the CD
seems to carry extremely heavy weight in comparison
to the others, but in actual fact the maximum value
of the CSC is 5.3 times the minimum, while the maximum CD is only 4.5 times the minimum. Thus changes
in social conditions would seem to offer a landowner
the greatest tax benefits.

On closer examination, it is possible to offer
a seemingly realistic rationale for the range of
values of the coefficients. But before suggesting
that rationale, it is necessary to equip the reader
with a fuller understanding of the derivation of the
coefficients.

The methods of calculation of the tax coefficients reveal much about the values of Brazilian
agrarian reform. The derivations of the CEY and the
CSC have been treated at length in Chapters 3 and 4.
It was demonstrated that the calculation of the CEY
placed high value upon productivity, income, investment, and businesslike attitude. The calculation of
the CSC emphasized owner-family operation and the
provision of housing, education, and justice to dependent people.

Coefficient of Dimension

Once the size of each property is stated in
modulos, each owner is assigned a number of modulos.
If a property is held by a single owner who has no
other rural properties, his assigned number of modulos is identical to the number of modulos assigned
to his property. In this case the CD is determined
simply by consulting a table (Table 23).

If the property is owned by a holder who has
other rural real estate or if the property is shared
among two or more holders, one of three more complex

methods must be applied. The first method applies
to the holder of two or more properties, who is
assigned a CD for each of his holdings, as determined by the number of modulos on each property and
the CD table. Each of these coefficients is then
weighted according to the percentage that the property it represents comprises of the total land held
by the owner. The weighted values are then added to
yield the composite Coefficient of Dimension, which
is assigned to both properties. By way of illustration (Table 24), let us assume that a holder of two
properties in Bragança Paulista has a total of 200
hectares, one property of 50 hectares devoted to
grazing and another of 150 hectares in perennial
crops. The former property would have one modulo,
so its CD would be 1.0, while the latter would have
ten modulos and a CD of 1.5. Since the first property comprises 25 per cent of the total area held,
its contribution to the composite CD is 0.2, 25 per
cent of 1.0. The contribution of the second property is 1.1, 75 per cent of 1.5. The composite CD,
then, is 1.3, and is assigned to each property. The
general effect of the application of this method is
to reduce the CD and therefore the tax rate on properties with larger numbers of modulos and to raise
the CD and the tax rate on those with fewer modulos.
Since the CD is progressive, an owner can reduce his
total tax by buying additional properties of certain
prescribed types. For example, he may buy a smaller
(in modulos) property with a lower-value land than
his original holding, and the CD of the smaller
property will reduce the CD assigned to the original
holding, thus reducing the tax rate and the taxes on
that property. The CD assigned to the smaller
property will be larger than it would otherwise, but
the resultant tax rate will be levied on lower-value
land. If the unimproved land value of the new,
smaller property is sufficiently lower than that of
the original, the total tax paid on both properties
will be smaller. A loophole such as this may well
impede progress toward Brazilian agrarian goals.

     In the case of a multiowned property, that is,
one shared by one or more holders, a second method
applies (Table 25), and a CD is determined for each
owner on the basis of his percentage share of the
property. This is done by multiplying the decimal
equivalent of his percentage of the property by the
total number of modulos contained in the property.
The resulting number of modulos assigned to each
holder is then translated into the owner's Coefficient of Dimension in accordance with the CD table.

TABLE 23

Modulo-Coefficient of Dimension Scale

Number of Modulos	Coefficient of Dimension
0.1 - 1.0	1.0
1.1 - 10	1.5
11 - 30	2.0
31 - 80	2.5
81 - 150	3.0
151 - 300	3.5
301 - 600	4.0
601 and over	4.5

TABLE 24

Calculating the CD for a Property Whose
Owner Holds More than One Property

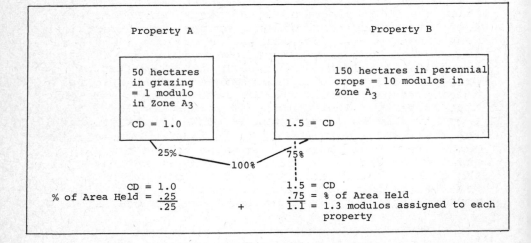

Property A

50 hectares
in grazing
= 1 modulo
in Zone A_3

CD = 1.0

25%   100%   75%

Property B

150 hectares in perennial
crops = 10 modulos in
Zone A_3

1.5 = CD

CD = 1.0
% of Area Held = .25
                 ____
                 .25   +

1.5 = CD
.75 = % of Area Held
____
1.1 = 1.3 modulos assigned to each
      property

Each of these coefficients is then multiplied by the decimal equivalent of each owner's percentage of the property and the products added to yield the CD for the holding. This method of calculation can, and often does, have the effect of producing a lower property CD than if the property were under a single owner. The method may be just and useful when it is applied to properties that are held and worked jointly, but it can also reduce taxes on land that is held by nonparticipating owners. Thus those properties in joint ownership at the time of the land survey are in a better tax position, insofar as the CD is concerned, than those held singly, even though mere joint ownership bears no obvious relationship to more effective farming. In actual fact, there appears to be a greater incidence of multi-ownership by nonparticipators than of properties held and worked in common. Further, it seems possible to reduce one's tax by merely assigning a percentage share of the property to dependent members of the family. Such a measure requires no change in farming methods, allocation of land, or investment, and in itself results in no increase in output nor wider distribution of income. Like the first alternate method, it seems to reduce the effectiveness of the tax system to bring about meaningful changes in farm operation.

The final method applies to properties that are held by more than one owner, any one of which holds all or part of another property (Table 26). This method of calculation of the CD seems even more unrealistic and its effect upon decision-making even more obscure. Each owner's CD enters into the computation in the same manner as in the second method, but for those who own or share in other properties, the individual CD is a product of the conditions on those other properties as well as the one to which the CD is being applied. Owners of the property in question receive premiums or are assigned penalties on the basis of size and use (since use enters into the calculation of modulos) conditions on properties over which they have no control. One need only consider the Brazilian institution of the extended family and past practices of land inheritance in order to realize the potential ramifications of such a method for calculating an important component of the land tax.

TABLE 25

Calculating the CD for a Property with Multi-Owners

Owner	Each Owner's % of This Property	Each Owner's Modulo	Each Owner's CD	Each Owner's % of This Property	Each Owner's % of CD
A	35.0	.350 x 10 = 3.5	= 1.5	x .350 =	.52
B	10.0	.100 x 10 = 1.0	= 1.0	x .100 =	.10
C	32.0	.320 x 10 = 3.2	= 1.5	x .320 =	.48
D	23.0	.230 x 10 = 2.3	= 1.5	x .230 =	.34
					1.44 or 1.4[a]

This Property Contains 10 Modulos.   This Property's CD Based on
With One Owner Its CD Would Be 1.5.   Multi-Ownership............ 1.4.

a CD's range from 1.0 to 4.5 in units of 0.5, but the CD's calculated
   for multiowned properties remain in units of 0.1.

TABLE 26

And if Some of the Above Owners Hold Other Properties

Owner				
A	3.5 = 1.5	x	.350	=	.52
B	1.0 = 1.0	x	.100	=	.10
C	11.0[a]= 2.0	x	.320	=	.64
D	11.2[b]= 2.0	x	.230	=	.46
					1.72 or 1.7[c]

This Property's CD Based On
Multi-Owners, Some With
Other Properties.......... 1.7

a Owner C is assigned 7.8 modulos from another property he owns and
   these are added to the 3.2 modulos he holds on this property to
   give him a total of 11.0 modulos.

b Owner D is assigned 8.9 modulos from another property he owns and
   these are added to the 2.3 modulos he holds on this property to
   give him a total of 11.2 modulos.

c CD's range from 1.0 to 4.5 in units of 0.5, but the CD's calculated for
   for multiowned properties remain in units of 0.1.

Coefficient of Location

The Coefficient of Location is an attempt to quantify the relative degree of access to markets for each of the rural properties in the system, proceeding from the realistic notion that properties with superior market access have higher economic potential. Superficially, it seems an expression of a desire to place a heavier share of the tax burden on holders who are best able to carry a heavier share. Examined more closely, it has a more meaningful implication and goal, which may be stated in the following manner: Those properties that have superior market access should be pushed to higher levels of production so they can better afford to pay the taxes levied. The practice of land speculation is widespread in the circumurban areas and in areas where the transportation infrastructure is most highly developed, which are precisely the areas where the greatest immediate gains in agriculture can be made. IBRA hopes that the CL will place enough of an additional burden on speculators that they will voluntarily give up land in such areas to more productive uses.

The CL has several component parts, the derivations of which are quite complex. Since these calculations add little to understanding the meaning and impact of the CL, the full description of its derivation is relegated to Appendix C. It is sufficient to indicate here that in a general fashion the CL varies directly with the market potential of the physiographic zone in which the property is located and the reliability of its routes of access, and varies inversely with the distance to its customary market. Note that none of these conditions can be modified by a given propertyholder, although the CL may guide his decision to buy or sell.

AN UNDERLYING RATIONALE

As indicated early in this chapter, it is possible to suggest a rationale underlying the tax system. While the Land Statute is nowhere explicit on this matter, the tax system seems to reflect several values of Brazilian agrarian reform. These values, or principles, can be stated simply. First, every rural landholder should participate in the

support of local public services; accordingly, no
combination of coefficients can result in a tax rate
of zero. This principle is relaxed in the exemption
from payment accorded owners meeting all the following requirements: (1) they must own no other rural
properties; (2) their holding must be less than 20
hectares in size, (3) the holding must be worked by
a single family. Secondly, as has been indicated,
the Land Statute places a high value on the family
farm unit; thus the lowest possible CD of 1.0
applies to farms with only one modulo. Persons
holding larger properties must pay for that privilege in the form of higher tax rates; the greater
the privilege enjoyed, the greater the rate of payment. Thirdly, propertyholders have an obligation
to use their land in ways that are consistent with
the public interest. This principle implies the
responsibility of those in control of the land resource to devote that resource to productive uses at
a high level of efficiency. Owners who meet this
responsibility at a satisfactory level of productivity are to be assigned a CEY of 1.0. Holders not
fully fulfilling this obligation are expected to
carry a larger share of the public finance burden
with their part of that load proportional to their
degree of default. On the other hand, landowners
who exceed society's expectations in their organization and use of the land resource are rewarded in
the form of reduced tax burdens. Fourthly, holders
who utilize the labors of others in the use of their
land have special obligations, including the provision of social services and "fair" returns to
these dependent people. Execution of these responsibilities at a satisfactory level results in a
CSC of 1.0. Default, total or partial, on these
duties results in a higher CSC, and, as a result, a
higher tax rate. Owners who are even more generous
in their relations with dependent people are rewarded through a reduction of their tax rates.

Finally, the potential for generating income
from the land varies with the market access of the
land. Owners who benefit most highly from the trans-
port infrastructure developed by society should pay
more heavily for the maintenance and extension of
that infrastructure. Accordingly, a CL of 1.0 is
assigned to those properties which benefit least and
a CL of 1.6 to those which benefit most. The tax
system, then, can be thought of as a formalization
of values related to the social and economic responsibilities of landholders.

It is tempting to regard the tax system as a tool in determining priority areas according to their economic and social health on the basis of a single summary measure, their average tax rates. At the outset, it seems logical that if properties were arranged in descending order of their tax rates, that those at the top of the array would constitute more serious problems for reform than those below, and areas with higher average tax rates might be assigned higher levels of priority for direct governmental action. This approach, however, can be seriously misleading. It is probable that latifundios will have high tax rates, but minifundios generally have rates that are much lower, since they seldom have as much as one modulo and as a result their CD's are always around 1.0. Thus areas with severe problems with both munifundios and latifundios may well have average tax rates somewhere around the national mean or median.

Nevertheless, two of the coefficients do have potential use beyond their function as tax rate components. The CSC and the CEY, taken separately, can be regarded as indicators of the nature of problems on a given holding or in specific areas. Many latifundios by use could be brought to respectable status by improvements in conditions that would give high magnitudes for either of these coefficients. Thus the coefficients themselves, which are measures of farm health, may at the same time suggest remedies for improving the state of health of the holding. Further, areas with high average levels of either of these coefficients may be assigned high priority for treatment aimed specifically at improving those problems indicated as most severe by the specific coefficient.

The revenue-generating function of the land tax and the potential use of the coefficients for assigning priorities and suggesting remedial action notwithstanding, probably the most crucial role played by the system of taxation is in forcing improvements in the rural sector within a structured set of guidelines. In a sense, the tax system is analagous to a game. The propertyholders are the players, IBRA is the referee, the rewards are reduced taxes, and the means of achieving those rewards are improvements in the economic and social conditions on the properties. One can refuse to play the game when it proves too strenuous or one's talents seem inappropriate by transfering one's property to

another player, either a new participant or one already in the game. The efficacy of the game in
achieving national goals is difficult to evaluate,
but such an assessment will be attempted here.

ASSESSMENT OF THE TAX SYSTEM

In order for a tax system to be effective in
forcing or guiding decisions within a general context of free enterprise, it must meet several conditions. First, the system must be comprehensible
to the decision-makers. In our case, the means of
achieving tax reductions must be clear to propertyholders. Secondly, the tax reductions must be
sufficiently great to justify the cost of achieving
them. Finally, the system should not contain contradictory or inconsistent elements. The Brazilian
land tax system has weaknesses with respect to the
first two conditions, and its adequacy in meeting
the last condition can be questioned.

As demonstrated earlier in this chapter, the
system of land taxation is extremely complex. Even
highly literate Brazilians should encounter difficulty in wading through the derivation of each of
the coefficients, and tracing the impact of changes
in the component parts of the coefficients is even
more difficult. Given the high rate of illiteracy
widely reported in rural Brazil (in most cases ex-
ceeding 50 per cent), it seems likely that the bulk
of the decision-makers will neither understand the
rules of the game nor be able to play it in such a
way as to aid in achieving the stated national goals.

In addition, the rewards for improvements are
insufficient to bring about change. It has been
shown that a holder can affect his CD and his CL
only through decisions to acquire or dispose of
land. Undoubtedly some decisions of this sort will
be made but such decisions do not change economic
or social conditions on a property in any direct
way. Thus the two strategic coefficients in effect-
ing change are the CEY and the CSC.

Superficially, each of these coefficients prom-
ises to force change. By reducing one's CEY from a
maximum of 1.5 to a minimum of 0.4, a reduction in
taxes of almost 74 per cent is achieved. A similar
change in the CSC, from 1.6 to 0.3, results in a

reduction in taxes of over 81 per cent. Changes from the maximum to the minimum values of both coefficients at the same time results in a tax reduction of 95 per cent. Nevertheless, when applied to actual properties, the tax benefits resulting from such changes seem woefully inadequate to act as incentives to propertyholders.

The inadequacy of possible tax benefits from these sources is especially clear in the case of the CSC. Tax data for 214 properties in the município of Bragança Paulista were analyzed to verify this contention. The analysis was based on the idea that in order for tax benefits to act as incentives, the cost of achieving these benefits must not exceed the resultant rewards. The data on each property include the four tax coefficients, the holding's land value, and its current tax. For each property a new tax was computed by replacing its actual CSC with a new value of 0.3. This new, hypothetical tax was then subtracted from the old to yield the tax saving that could be made by reducing the CSC to its lowest possible value.

Since no information about the cost of such changes is available, it was necessary to use one of the assumptions in the reform system to make reasonable estimates of this element. In arriving at a useful definition of a modulo, IBRA assumes that such a unit must be capable of supporting four working adults at minimum salaries, must be capable of providing a 15 per cent return to both land and capital, and must also be capable of generating an additional 1.6 minimum salaries (0.4 minimum salaries for each of 4 laborers) so that the owner can discharge his social responsibilities to his family and his workers. This last requirement was used in estimating the cost of making social changes. Since the minimum annual salary in Bragança Paulista was Cr$792,000[2] at the time of the survey, the annual cost of reducing the CSC from its maximum (1.6) to its minimum (0.3) was postulated at Cr$316,800 per laborer (0.4 times the annual minimum salary). This was the figure used to calculate a cost per unit of reduction in the CSC, with its thirteen units between 0.3 and 1.6. It was assumed that the cost of reducing the CSC from one level to the next is constant; that is, that the cost of reducing the CSC from 1.6 to 1.5 is the same as from 1.5 to 1.4, from 1.4 to 1.3, and so on. Thus the per unit cost of reduction in the CSC was postulated at approximately Cr$24,000 per laborer per year. The total cost of reducing the CSC from its actual value to the minimum value was calculated for each property in the following way. The minimum value, 0.3, was subtracted from the actual CSC. This difference was then multiplied by ten in order to determine the number of reduction units possible. This value was then multiplied by the product of the number of laborers and the cost per unit of reduction per laborer. Stated mathematically:

ESTIMATED TOTAL COST OF REDUCTION =
$$(CSÇ - 0.3) \times 10 \times (Cr\$316,000/13) \times \text{NO. OF LABORERS}$$

The potential tax benefits were then compared to the estimated costs of achieving the benefits. In <u>none</u> of the 214 cases did the benefit exceed the cost.

In order to provide additional support for these findings, another set of costs was estimated. This set was also based upon IBRA assumptions regarding the definition of the modulo, but since it is possible for a holder to employ more or fewer than four laborers per modulo the costs were estimated by the following formula:

ESTIMATED TOTAL COST =
$$(CSC - 0.3) \times 10 \times (Cr\$1,267,200/13) \times \text{NO. OF MODULOS.}$$

Where Cr$1,267,200 is that part of a modulo's income postulated by IBRA to allow the holder to discharge his social responsibilities.

The result of comparing this set of costs (per modulo) with the corresponding tax benefits was essentially the same as in the first set (per laborer). While some owners suffered a smaller net loss than on the basis of the first set, others suffered larger net losses. In no case was the tax saving greater than the cost of the social improvements.

Theoretically, it can be demonstrated that the larger the other three coefficients, the greater the absolute tax benefit from reductions in the CSC. It can also be demonstrated that larger properties that utilize few workers and have high-value land can probably realize net gains through the reduction of the CSC, because of their large taxable base and the few workers for which they have responsibility. In fact, the costly social responsibilities demanded of the owner by the CSC may encourage owners to

substitute machinery for labor. This may be a com-
mendable economic goal, but if that is what Brazil
wants, it could be achieved in more direct, more
effective ways. And such a goal may be less com-
mendable from a broader national viewpoint. For
example, the CSC is viewed by many as a tool for
slowing the movement from farm to city. To the degree that it stimulates mechanization, it will ac-
celerate this movement. For practical purposes,
unless the assumptions of this analysis are totally
unrealistic, or the Bragança sample is far from
representative of the Brazilian condition, the CSC
bears little promise of generating social improvement in rural Brazil.

     It was not possible to submit the CEY to the
same kind of test. While this coefficient is given
for each of the properties, the cost of reducing it
could not be estimated reasonably from data available. It can be shown that potential absolute tax
savings through CEY reduction in the Bragança sample
are small, but implied in the reduction of the CEY
are additional benefits accruing directly from improved crop yields and more efficient management.
The small potential tax saving possible from such
improvements just might provide the additional incentive for a holder to improve the use of his land
in anticipation of increased income. Verification
of this hypothesis requires further analysis of the
cost-benefit relationships involved. But the Land
Inventory does not provide sufficient data for such
a study.

     In any case, further examination of the tax
system and its application to Brazil provides over-
whelming evidence that the resultant taxes are just
too low to be very effective, either in guiding decisions or in generating revenues. The highest
possible rural tax rate in Brazil, stemming from the
highest possible coefficient product (17.2), is 3.45
per cent (Table 27). The lowest rate, resulting
from a coefficient product of 0.12, is 0.02 per cent.
If all four of a property's coefficients are 1.0,
the constant (.002) will, of course, be its tax rate.

     The constant of .002 is set forth in the Land
Statute, but its derivation is nowhere made clear.
Whatever the origin, it is simply low to the point
of insignificance. It is difficult to believe that
in setting such a low level the framers of the Land

TABLE 27

The Development of Selected Tax Rates

	CD	CL	CSC	CEY	Product	Constant	Rate
Highest Coefficient Level	4.5 x	1.6 x	1.6 x	1.5 =	17.280 x	.002 =	.03456
Lowest Coefficient Level	1.0 x	1.0 x	0.3 x	0.4 =	.120 x	.002 =	.00024
All Coefficients At 1.0	1.0 x	1.0 x	1.0 x	1.0 =	1.000 x	.002 =	.00200

Statute deliberately chose to weaken the tax as a
weapon in agrarian reform, or that they were so unrealistic as to believe that by starting low they
could later raise the level without real question.
They may have settled on a low constant to head off
any direct and immediate opposition, under the
assumption that the coefficient product whose level
is set by the property owner's answers on the questionnaire would yield a "respectable" tax rate per
property. The mean tax rates for physiographic
zones suggest how unjustified such an assumption
was (Figure 8, Tables 28 and 29). Not one of those
mean tax rates even approaches the extreme rate
that, at that, is only 3.45 per cent of a property's
unimproved land value. At the other end of the
scale, the .002 (0.2 per cent) constant is not even a
"floor," as the mean tax rate for two physiographic
zones (Alto Purus, Acre and Mucuri, Minas Gerais)
attests. Not only is the mean for all physiographic
zones low (0.303) but more than half the 228 zones
fall below this mean (median = 0.280). True, the
distribution is skewed to the right (the higher
levels), but this scarcely heralds even moderately
high tax rates for many properties.

     Clearly, the coefficient product does not make
up for this very low constant, and the result is an
altogether too low tax rate. By comparison, Thomas
Carroll calls the 0.4% "standard rate" for rural
land in Columbia light.[3] Carroll is not clear in
stating whether this standard is a mean, a base, or
simply the rate most often applied. What is clear
is that it is well above Brazil's lowest potential
rate (.02 per cent) and a point higher than the
mean for Brazil's 228 physiographic zones. And if
0.4 per cent is a mean for Colombia, only ten zones
in all of Brazil are above it.

     The Currie report on Colombian land reform
calls for a base rate of 0.4% on well-used land and
higher rates on poorly used lands,[4] a very high tax
rate in Brazilian terms. Unlike Colombia, Brazil
has succeeded in setting up and completing the com-
prehensive land inventory necessary for levying a
regressive tax based on differences among the land
parcels. Regressive though it may be, the present
Brazilian tax rate is probably too low even to evoke
a response from affected landholders.

FIGURE 8

Distribution of Mean Tax Rates by Physiographic Zone

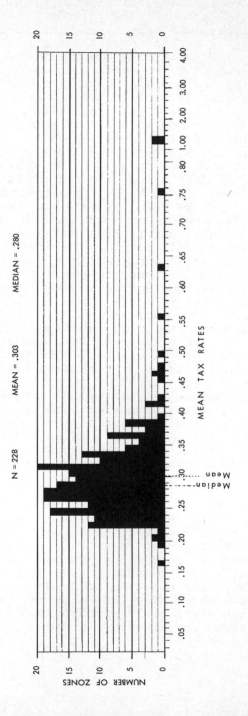

TABLE 28

Twelve Zones with Lowest Mean Tax Rates

(Zones with mean tax rates below .229--more than
two standard deviations below the mean for all
physiographic zones.)

	Zone	Mean Product of the Four Coefficients	No. of Properties	Mean Size in Ha.
1.	.168 Alto Purús, Acre	.81	1,614	265
2.	.198 Mucuri, Minas Gerais	.99	17,620	113
3.	.206 Alto Uruguai, Rio Grande do Sul	1.03	111,825	21
4.	.208 Sertão Alto, Paraíba	1.04	7,278	27
5.	.213 Cacaueira, Bahia	1.06	20,433	70
6.	.222 Sertão do Araripe, Pernambuco	1.11	9,993	71
7.	.222 Itacambira, Minas Gerais	1.11	26,285	71
8.	.223 Médio Jequitinhonha, Minas Gerais	1.11	12,447	173
9.	.225 Recôncavo, Bahia	1.12	17,397	35
10.	.228 Norte, Espírito Santo	1.14	16,691	65
11.	.228 Andradina, São Paulo	1.14	5,117	80
12.	.228 Sertão do Alto Moxotó, Pernambuco	1.14	3,460	121

TABLE 29

Twenty-Three Zones with Highest Mean Tax Rates

(Zones with mean tax rates above .377--more
than two standard deviations above the
mean for all physiographic zones.)

Mean Rate	Zone	Mean Product of the Four Coefficients	No. of Properties	Mean Size in Ha.
1. 1.342	Mazagão, Amapa	6.71	139	1,650
2. 1.273	Arapuanã, Mato Grosso	6.36	55	10,900
3. .756	Tapajós, Pará	3.78	356	870
4. .630	Chapada, Mato Grosso	3.15	6,944	2,120
5. .563	Encosta Norte, Mato Grosso	2.81	1,826	920
6. .499	Litoral Santos, São Paulo	2.49	451	215
7. .468	Campos Gerais, Paraná	2.34	18,822	62
8. .466	Litoral, Paraná	2.33	2,441	177
9. .454	Rio Purus, Amazonas	2.27	1,053	1,180
10. .446	Curitiba, Paraná	2.23	31,652	17
11. .427	Catrimâni, Roraima	2.13	347	658
12. .417	São Paulo, São Paulo	2.08	25,509	31
13. .413	Alto Ivaí, Paraná	2.06	22,407	41
14. .413	Campos d'Oeste, Paraná	2.06	13,184	124
15. .395	Oiapoque, Amapá	1.97	22	139
16. .388	Iratí, Paraná	1.94	28,985	17
17. .387	Médio Parnaíba, Maranhão	1.93	4,066	215
18. .384	Planalto, Piauí	1.92	4,813	243
19. .381	Alto Ribeira, Paraná	1.90	7,358	67
20. .381	Castro, Paraná	1.90	6,147	63
21. .380	Juruá, Amazonas	1.90	260	2,150
22. .379	Gurupí, Pará	1.89	227	261
23. .378	Solimões Javari, Amazonas	1.89	435	1,060

The Pattern of Tax Rates

At least part of the pattern of zones with very high and very low mean tax rates can be attributed to factors of size (CD), location (CL), and use (CEY). (See Figure 9). With but one exception, high mean tax rates characterize zones in the upper Amazon basin and probably stem from the large (over 800 hectares) mean property size of each. Rural properties held for recreational and/or speculative purposes doubtless contribute to the high mean tax rate in the litorals of São Paulo and Paraná and in zones around the capital cities of these states. Low or nonexistent agricultural productivity on many of these properties yields a very high CEY, and because these zones contain large urban populations, they have both a high mean CL and a high market potential. This high market potential is expressed in numerous modulos per property and a resultant high CD, despite the fact that the mean property size in these zones is not large. Less apparent are those conditions that produce so high a mean tax rate in the other seven zones of Paraná state.

The low mean tax rate in Alto Purús, Acre, may result from the dominance of planned agricultural settlements. But far to the south, in Alto Uruguai, Rio Grande do Sul, efficient middle-range holdings, some of them parts of planned settlements, are deteriorating. Here long-continued subdivision of farms owned by non-Luso Europeans has created more than 111,000 holdings. This dominance of minifundios (mean size in the zone is 21 hectares), coupled with still fair but deteriorating social and economic conditions, yields a very low mean tax rate. Indeed, with such a small mean property size, as many as eighty to ninety thousand of these potentially productive units may contain twenty or fewer hectares and thus be exempt from the tax. This is ironic and dismaying, for here property size, not the intangible human factors, is the chief drawback to a viable agriculture and payment of the tax. Principally because of this "minifundioization," IBRA has declared the entire state of Rio Grande do Sul to be one of Brazil's five agricultural "priority areas." Article 34 of the Land Statute gives IBRA this power and specifies the kinds of public commitments it can make in order to revitalize the agricultural environment. A similar

kind of minifundioization and low CD's may be responsible for the low mean tax rates in the zones
of the Minas Gerais-Bahia-Espírito Santo "corner"
and in the sertões of Pernambuco and Paraíba.

Land Value and the Tax

The third factor in Brazil's Rural Land Tax,
the unimproved value of the property, does little to
make the total tax per holding respectable. Each
owner declares his unimproved property value on his
questionnaire. The more sophisticated try not to
overvalue for obvious reasons, but they also fear
undervaluing in the event of expropriation for value.
IBRA also attempts to prevent undervaluing by setting a minimum value per hectare in each physiographic zone, ranging from Cr$5,000 (US$2.50)[5] per
hectare in three zones in Acre and Roraima to
Cr$155,000 (US$77.50) in the zones around the cities
of São Paulo and Rio de Janeiro (Figures 9 and 10).
The mean for the 228 zones (and therefore for
Brazil) is Cr$27,100 (US$13.25) per hectare. The
Bragança Paulista base is Cr$81,000 (US$40.50),
three times the Brazil mean and fifth highest in the
country, a position shared with Litoral de Santos
around the Paulista port city and Baixada de Guandú
in the state of Rio de Janeiro just outside the city
of Rio. These latter two are on urban peripheries
where agricultural uses compete with potential urban,
industrial, and recreational uses. Bragança is
spatially just on the fringe of this kind of com-
petition, perhaps only a few years away from direct
involvement.

Multiplying the mean tax rate for a zone by the
IBRA-set minimum land value per hectare for that
zone shows just how negligible land value is in
raising the tax on a property (Table 30).

One must use care in analyzing these figures,
for while the mean tax rate probably reflects fairly
accurately the aggregate of conditions in a zone,
there is no way of telling how many properties are
listed above the minimum value per hectare by their
owners or how many are set at base by IBRA because
their owners undervalue them. (Although not available for Braganca Paulista zone, this information is
available for Braganca Paulista município and will
be dealt with in detail in the next chapter.) It

FIGURE 9

Physiographic Zones with Very High and Very Low Tax Rates

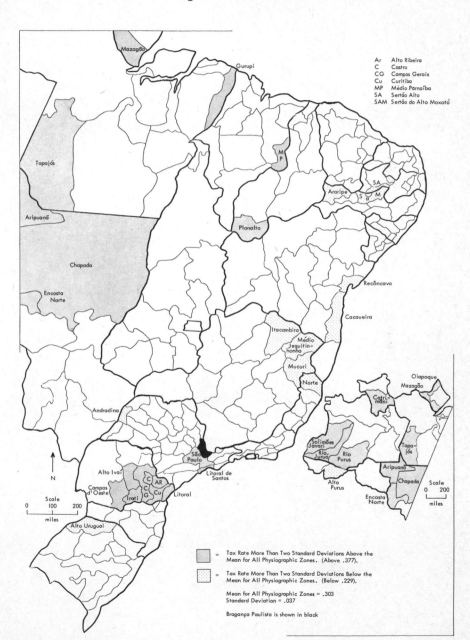

Ar   Alto Ribeira
C   Castro
CG   Campos Gerais
Cu   Curitiba
MP   Médio Parnaíba
SA   Sertão Alto
SAM Sertão do Alto Moxotó

= Tax Rate More Than Two Standard Deviations Above the Mean for All Physiographic Zones. (Above .377).

= Tax Rate More Than Two Standard Deviations Below the Mean for All Physiographic Zones. (Below .229).

Mean for All Physiographic Zones = .303
Standard Deviation = .037

Bragança Paulista is shown in black

FIGURE 10

IBRA-Set Unimproved Land Values by
Physiographic Zone

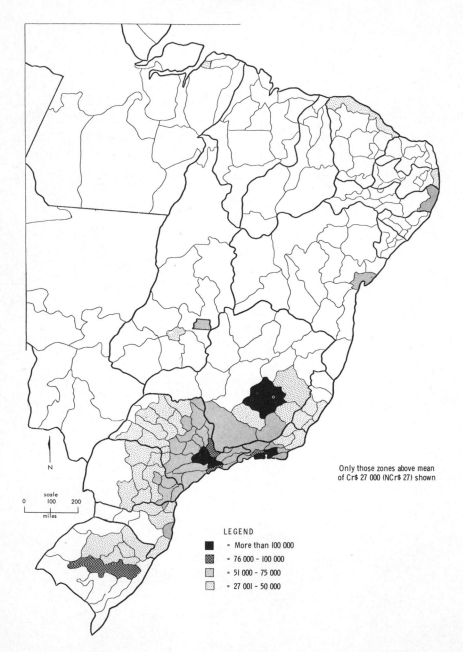

Only those zones above mean
of Cr$ 27 000 (NCr$ 27) shown

LEGEND

■ = More than 100 000

▨ = 76 000 - 100 000

▧ = 51 000 - 75 000

▒ = 27 001 - 50 000

scale
0   100   200
miles

N

is apparent, however, that even if every one of the
São Paulo zone's properties were listed at ten times
this highest base value in the country (Cr$155,000),
each property would still be taxed an average of
only US$3.20 per hectare.

TABLE 30

Mean Tax per Hectare on the Minimum
Unimproved Land Value for Selected Zones

Zone	Mean Rate	Minimum Unimproved Land Value per Hectare	Mean Tax on the Minimum Value per Hectare
Bragança Paulista	.00348	Cr$81,000 US$40.50	Cr$282 US$0.14
São Paulo	.00417	Cr$155,000 US$77.50	Cr$646 US$0.32
Guanabara	.00303	Cr$155,000 US$77.50	Cr$469 US$0.23
Mazagão Amapá	.01342	Cr$6,000 US$3.00	Cr$80 US$0.04

   Suffice it to say that if not in São Paulo then
nowhere will the land value submitted by the property owner compensate the low tax rate sufficiently
to yield a respectable tax per hectare of rural
property. Certainly not in Bragança Paulista zone,
where if the moderately high mean tax rate is
applied to the base land value, the tax is only
US$0.14 per hectare, and if applied to ten times the
base, still only US$1.40. There is no evidence that
IBRA has deliberately set a low land-value base in
circumurban areas in order to protect small farmers
from being forced through taxes to sell their lands
to urban speculators and developers.

   The size of the holding, of course, determines
the total tax on a property, and this could constitute a real burden. But where tax per hectare
tends to be higher, land parcels tend to be smaller.
Holdings average 31 hectares in both Bragança
Paulista and São Paulo zones, so the average tax on
a property in the former is Cr$8,742 (US$4.37) and
in the latter Cr$20,026 (US$10.01). This means that
75 acres of land (31 hectares) are taxed at an average of 5.7 cents (U.S.) per acre in Bragança Paulista zone and at 12.4 cents (U.S.) per acre in São
Paulo zone.

Very simply put, the tax is too low. But were it higher, it might hurt the very small owner-operator whose output is near subsistence and thereby force him into a rural labor or, worse, urban slum situation. It might even do this without at the same time being high enough to force the nonagricultural landowner (one who holds land for psychosocial or inflation-combatting reasons, but neither lives nor works on it) to either invest in the property or reallocate its existing resources to meet the tax or bring it down.

There is another possible advantage to low taxes. They could mean a higher percentage of easier collections, with the result that taxes paid by 3.5 million properties would accumulate to a very large sum. The federal government could then make much of this tax money available in concentrated doses to those zones of municípios where the rural situation is socially explosive or on the threshold of economic viability--to IBRA's "priority areas," for example--and these doses shifted among regions as their needs dictate. Unfortunately, to set up such a system would take a change in the Land Statute, whose Article 43 specifies that tax receipts belong to the município where they are collected. (IBRA officials say these moneys form an agricultural loan pool, but the Statute is silent on this matter.) Thus even if all taxes are collected, given the low Rural Land Tax, how much money could possibly be available in a single municipio for agricultural loans or any other purpose?

Potential Contradictions

That a tax system of the sort outlined in the Land Statute should not contain contradictory elements is obvious. Actions designed to achieve one goal should not work against the achievement of other goals. For the most part, the Brazilian system seems to be free of such contradictions, except in one significant instance.

Again the problem involves the CSC and the CEY. It is possible, and even probable, that the CEY responds rather readily to capital inputs into directly productive means. This response is largely attributable to increased crop yields, which improve two components of the CEY. The Agricultural Yields Factor is improved directly through increased crop and/or livestock yields, and the Economic Yields Factor is improved by the consequent rise in income.

Now the CSC can also be improved through increased capital inputs, but these inputs must be channeled into the provision of social needs, and thus into uses which are not likely to affect economic conditions on the property in any significant way.

The implications of these relationships seems clear. A propertyholder who attempts to save in taxes by investing in social conditions may well be diverting capital from directly productive uses, thus affecting both his farm income and his CEY adversely. Even if there is not net reduction in capital devoted to directly productive activities on the property in question, the new capital must come from some source. In a capital-poor country, the practice of this type of social investment is questionable, but social justice is an immediate Brazilian goal and Brazilians must judge its level of priority. The authors' comments are intended to help clarify the problems involved in such a choice.

The Rural Land Tax system must be judged to have serious weaknesses. It is too complex to be understood by a vast majority of rural holders. The resultant taxes are too low, and the ranges between the highest and the lowest possible levels are too narrow. These facts seem to indicate that the tax will be ineffective in generating public revenues, and more importantly, that it is inadequate to cause holders to make changes for the purpose of achieving tax reductions.

NOTES

1. In a sense the Coefficient of Dimension may also be thought of as a classifier, since any property having a CD of 4.5 is classed a latifundio by size.

2. All Brazilian monetary values in this book are in old cruzeiros, which were in effect at the time of the Land Inventory.

3. Thomas F. Carroll, "The Land Reform Issue in Latin America," Latin American Issues, Essay and Comments, ed. Albert O. Hirschman (New York: The Twentieth Century Fund, 1961), p. 192.

4. Ibid.

    5. All cruzeiro-to-dollar conversions in this
book are based on a 1966 average of 2,000 cruzeiros
per U.S. dollar unless otherwise specified.

CHAPTER **6** PROPERTY TYPES: AN
ASSESSMENT OF THE
CLASSIFICATION SYSTEM IN
BRAGANÇA PAULISTA

A basic tenet of Brazil's land reform scheme is
that the nation's land resource can and should be
used in such ways as insure greater availabilities
of rural produce and higher rural incomes. Further,
these goals are to be accomplished within the constraints of wider distribution of the income generated from the land and higher levels of social justice. Owners are encouraged to make decisions about
the use of their land that are consistent with
these goals. The encouragement takes the form of
differential taxation and the threat of expropriation or other abridgments of the right of private
property. In order to apply these measures in an
effective way, each existing property must be judged
according to the degree to which its holder's
actions are consistent with the stated goals. The
preceding chapters have been devoted to description
of the Brazilian system of property classification
and taxation--that is, the methods by which each
property is judged and assessed. Any meaningful
assessment of the classification system should
attempt to determine the degree to which the complex
measures of the Brazilian system really separate
the properties into distinct groups. It is to this
question that this chapter is addressed.

That IBRA has successfully classified each
holding on the basis of the measures defined in
Brazilian land-reform legislation, there seems
little doubt. The levels of the CEY, CSC, and
other measures that act as disqualifiers from respectable status are established by law made by
Brazilians addressing themselves to a Brazilian
problem, and presumably reflect Brazilian values.
The authors take these measures as given and make
no attempt, at this juncture, to sit in judgment

upon them. Rather, an attempt is made to assess the
degree to which empresas rurais, latifundios, and
minifundios, as defined by the Brazilian system, are
truly distinct groups of properties in terms other
than those used as criteria in the IBRA classification system.

This attempt takes the form of statistical
tests of property data form Bragança Paulista,
designed to determine whether empresas rurais, minifundios, and latifundios constitute separate statistical populations with respect to variables (some of
which are factors in IBRA coefficients) derived from
the data on the individual properties.

There are a number of implications possible
from such an approach. The property data tested
concern characteristics of propertyholders, tenure
relationships, and decisions about the use of the
property, and the results of these conditions as
reflected in outputs. If empresas rurais, as a
group, can be shown to exhibit characteristics that
seem to be desirable by widely accepted criteria of
rural land use, and if, in addition, they form a
distinct population with definite owner and tenure
characteristics, perhaps it will be possible to more
clearly understand agricultural development in
Brazil.

                        THE DATA

The basic information-collection instrument
used by IBRA is the Land Inventory Questionnaire.
Information provided by propertyholders in completing
the questionnaires is printed on standard IBRA file
cards, one for each property, along with the average
modulos, the property's classification, the tax
coefficients, and the computed tax. The authors had
access to all the property cards for the entire
município of Bragança Paulista. The number of variables on each card was 137, and the number of properties was 1,980, so the total number of original
data items was approximately 250,000. Because an
exhaustive analysis of a matrix of this size would
be too expensive and timeconsuming, information was
discarded that was felt to be of little relevance to
the task at hand, and even then it was necessary to
resort to sampling. The ideal sample, perhaps, would
be stratified by property type with an equal percentage of each class--empresa rural, minifundio,

and latifundio--but the fact that Braganca municipio
had only 59 empresas rurais, while latifundios and
minifundios numbered approximately 300 and 1,600,
precluded this type of sampling. Any equal-percent-
age sample including a reasonably large number of
empresas rurais would defeat the purpose of sam-
pling--that is, to reduce the number of total cases
to manageable size. As a result, it was decided to
include in the sample all empresas rurais, 24 per
cent of the latifundios, and 5 per cent of the minifundios, so that the initial sample was made up of
59 empresas rurais, 70 latifundios, and 85 minifundios, 214 cases in all. Samples from the last two
classes were selected at random. Later, due to
obvious inconsistencies in individual responses or
lack of responses to critical questions, the sample
was cut for some purposes to 186 cases--50 empresas,
62 latifundios, and 74 minifundios. Little seems
to have been lost in this sampling process, since
the analysis is in terms of characteristics by class
and does not treat the 186 cases as though they com-
prised a single population.

     From this original data matrix were derived a
number of other measures, principally density measures or other ratios. The original and derived
variables are listed in Table 31.

     Despite the large number of items in the Land
Inventory questionnaire, there are serious deficiencies in the data. Net income and out-of-pocket
costs are conspicuously absent, and no statement of
man-days of labor or labor costs was supplied. Nor
is it possible from information provided to make a
reasonable estimate of these, of annual investment,
or of annual net income. Nevertheless, although
the data used in the analysis have their shortcom-
ings, they comprise the most complete body of prop-
erty-by-property information available for a
Brazilian municipio. It is hoped that, used with
care, this information can provide answers with
some approximation to reality.

              THE ANALYSIS' STRATEGY AND METHODS

     The strategy of the analysis involves the con-
struction and test of a general null hypothesis,
which states that the Brazilian system of land
classification does not differentiate properties

into separate populations with respect to the variables being tested. This hypothesis is then put in more specific form for each test. When a specific null hypothesis can be rejected, then each property type can be assigned a characteristic on the basis of its score in that variable.

The choice of statistical tests was guided by the scale of the variable being tested. The three property categories represent a nominal scale, while the variables, as shown in Table 31, include all three scales, interval, ordinal, and nominal. The variables of interval scale were subjected to difference-of-means tests. The variables of nominal scale were tested by Chi-square, and ordinal-scale variables were converted to nominal scale and also tested by Chi-square. The results of the tests are summarized in Tables 32 and 33.

Following the two examples below is an analysis of the results of each test.

TEST 1. DIFFERENCE OF MEANS[1]
  LEVEL OF MEASUREMENT: Gross Income per hectare, an interval scale.
  MODEL: $\sigma_{ER} \neq \sigma_{LAT}$
  NULL HYPOTHESIS: $M_{ER} \neq M_{LAT}$
  ALTERNATE HYPOTHESIS 1: Empresas rurais as a class produce higher gross incomes per hectare than do latifundios.
  ALTERNATE HYPOTHESIS 2: Latifundios as a class produce higher gross incomes per hectare than do empresas rurais.

TEST STATISTIC: t computed by the formula:

$$t = \frac{X_{ER} - X_{LAT}}{\sqrt{\dfrac{S^2_{ER}}{N_{ER}-1} + \dfrac{S^2_{LAT}}{N_{LAT}-1}}}$$

SIGNIFICANCE LEVEL AND CRITICAL REGION: .05 level of significance in a one-tailed test.

TABLE 31

Variables Tested for Bragança Paulista Sample

Tested by Difference of Means

1. Capital applied per hectare of useable land
2. Gross income per hectare of useable land
3. Total number of laborers
4. Capital applied per laborer
5. Gross income per laborer
6. Total useable land
7. Land value per hectare
8. Total capital applied
9. Number of wage laborers
10. Laborers per hectare
11. Percentage of land in coffee
12. Percentage of land in corn
13. Percentage of land in cattle
14. Percentage of land in rice
15. Percentage of land in forest
16. Percentage of land in beans
17. Percentage of land in specialty crops
18. Percentage of land under the owner's direct use
19. Technical level

Tested by Chi-Square

1. Resident owner
2. Owner administrator
3. Multi-property ownership
4. Common ownership through inheritance
5. Educational level
6. Foreign-born owner
7. Owner with other remunerative activity
8. Multi-owned property
9. Sharecropping on property
10. Tenancy on property
11. Wage labor used on property

TABLE 32

Results of Difference-of-Means Tests on 19 Variables,
Bragança Paulista Sample

Variable	ER vs. Min	ER vs. Lat	Min vs. Lat	Order of Mean
1. Capital/hectare of useable land	*	*		ER,Min,Lat
2. Gross income/hectare of useable land		*	*	Min,ER,Lat
3. Total laborers	*	*	*	ER,Lat,Min
4. Capital/laborer	*	*	*	ER,Min,Lat
5. Gross income/laborer	*	*		ER,Min,Lat
6. Total Useable Land	*	*	*	ER,Lat,Min
7. Land Value/hectare			*	Min,ER,Lat
8. Total Capital Applied	*	*	*	ER,Lat,Min
9. Wage Laborers	*	*	*	ER,Lat,Min
10. Laborers/hectare	*	*	*	Min,ER,Lat
11. % land in coffee	*	*		ER,Min,Lat
12. % land in corn				Lat,Min,ER
13. % land in cattle		*		Lat,Min,ER
14. % land in rice				Min,Lat,ER
15. % land in forest	*	*		ER,Lat,Min
16. % land in beans	*	*		Min,Lat,ER
17. % land in specialty crops	*			Min,Lat,ER
18. % land under direct use of owner				ER,Min,Lat
19. Technical Level	*	*	*	ER,Lat,Min

* Indicates t significant beyond .05 level.

TABLE 33

Partial Summary of Results of Chi-Square Tests on 11
Variables--Bragança Paulista

Variable	Property Types	Remarks
Tenancy	All possible combinations	None significant at .05 level
Sharecropping	All possible combinations	None significant at .05 level
Common owner- ship through inheritance	All possible combinations	None significant at .05 level
Owns other property	All possible combinations	None significant at .05 level
Owner administers	All possible combinations	None significant at .05 level
Owner resides on property	All possible combinations	None significant at .05 level
National origin	ER vs others	Significant at .05 level with ER having greater than expected frequency of foreign born
	All other combinations	None significant at .05 level
Educational level	ER-Min-Lat	Significant at .05 level with ER higher frequency at higher educational levels
	ER & others	Same as above
	ER-Min	Same as above
	ER-Lat	Same as above
Single ownership	ER-Min-Lat	Significant at .05 level with ER greater than expected frequency in multi-ownership
Other remunerative activity	ER & others	Significant at .05 level with ER greater than expected frequency in other remunerative activity
Wage laborers	ER-Min-Lat	Significant at .05 level with ER greater than expected
	ER & others	Same as above
	Lat & Min	Significant at .05 level with Lat greater than expected frequency

DEGREES OF FREEDOM: Since it is assumed that $\sigma_{ER} \neq \sigma_{LAT}$ the degrees of freedom are estimated from the formula:

$$df = \frac{\left[S_{ER}^2 / (N_{ER} - 1) + S_{LAT}^2 / (N_{LAT} - 1) \right]^2}{\left[S_{ER}^2 / (N_{ER} - 1) \right]^2 1/(N_{ER} + 1) + \left[S_{LAT}^2 / (N_{LAT} - 1) \right]^2 1/(N_{LAT} + 1)} \qquad -2$$

Note that the degrees of freedom can never exceed the number of cases in the sample. The general effect of this method is to reduce the number of degrees of freedom; thus the level of significance required is more difficult to obtain.

THE DATA:

	EMPRESAS	LATIFUNDIOS
N	50	62
$\overline{X}$	Cr$170,019	Cr$25,943
S	Cr$386,016	Cr$32,006

RESULTS:

t = 2.6541
df = 55

DECISION: Since a t-score of 2.6541 with 55 degrees of freedom is significant beyond the .05 level in a one-tailed test, the Null Hypothesis is rejected. Further, because the mean for empresas rurais is the higher mean, Alternate Hypothesis 1 is accepted and the characteristic of high gross income per hectare is assigned to empresas rurais. It must be noted, however, that "high" is used as a relative term within the limited universe of empresas rurais and latifundios based on a sample from Bragança Paulista.

TEST 2. CHI-SQUARE

LEVEL OF MEASUREMENT: Property type and whether or not wage labor is used on the property. Both are nominal scales.

NULL HYPOTHESIS: There is no difference between empresas rurais and latifundios in respect to the question of whether wage labor is used on the respective properties.

ALTERNATE HYPOTHESIS 1: Empresas rurais are more likely to use wage labor than are latifundios.

ALTERNATE HYPOTHESIS 2: Latifundios are more likely to use wage labor than are empresas.

TEST STATISTIC: Chi-square computed by the following formula:

$$\text{Chi-square} = \sum \frac{f_o^2}{fe} - N$$

LEVEL OF SIGNIFICANCE: .05

THE DATA:

Property Type	Use Wage Labor	Do Not Use Wage Labor	Total
E.R.	46	13	59
Lat.	22	44	66
Total	68	57	125

COMPUTATIONS: The first step is to compute the expected frequencies, based on the assumption that if there is no difference between the two property types with respect to the variable being tested, the types should share in the total wage-labor frequency in proportion to the percentage that each type represents of the total number of properties. Since the empresas rurais are 59 of 125 properties, they should be 59/125, or 47.2 per cent, of the properties that use wage labor. The expected frequency of wage-labor use for empresas rurais, then, is .472 x 68 (the total number of properties that use wage labor), or 32.1. The other expected frequencies are given in the following expanded contingency table.

Property Type	Use Wage Labor		Do Not Use Wage Labor		Total
E.R.	32.1	46	26.9	13	59
Lat.	35.9	22	30.1	44	66
Total	68		57		125

RESULTS:

$$\text{Chi-square} = 24.97$$
$$\text{degrees of freedom} = 1$$

DECISION: Since a Chi-square of 24.97 is significant beyond the .05 level, the Null Hypothesis
is rejected. Further, since the observed frequency for empresas rurais in the use of wage
labor is greater than the expected, Alternate
Hypothesis 1 is accepted, and the use of wage
labor is assigned as an attribute that differ-
entiates empresas from latifundios--subject,
of course, to the qualifications noted in
Test 1.

DIFFERENCES BETWEEN PROPERTY TYPES

The results of the statistical tests provide no
single answer to the central question posed earlier
in this chapter. In many of the variables tested,
the test statistic indicates a significant difference between the property types of the Brazilian
classification system, while for other variables no
significant difference is demonstrated. Nevertheless, it is possible to indicate the ways in which
the various types of property do differ from each
other, and some of the nondifferences prove instruc-
tive enough to be included as well.

The thirty variables tested may be arranged in
four sets: (1) those describing the owner; (2)
those describing the land; (3) those reflecting the
decisions of the owner in the use of the land; (4)
those resulting from the composite effects of the
first three sets. It should be noted that there is
possible overlapping among the first three sets.

For example, that an owner is resident upon the
property in question might be a characteristic of
the owner or could be thought of as a decision about
land use. The actual groupings are arbitrary,
guided by a desire to schematize the productive process, from owner-characteristics, through quality
and quantity of land resource under the owner's control, through his decisions on land use, to the
ultimate objective, output. The reader may well
choose different groupings.

Owner Attributes

     Eight variables are listed under the heading
"Owner Attributes." All of these variables are of
nominal scale, so Chi-square was the test applied.
In four of the variables, the test statistic was not
significant at the .05 level. Thus there appears to
be no significant difference among empresas rurais,
latifundios, and minifundios in the incidence of (1)
resident owners; (2) owner-administrators; (3) multi-
property ownership; (4) common ownership through
inheritance. Stated more precisely, none of the
three property types is more likely than the others
to have owners who live on the property, who administer the property, who own other properties, or who
hold the property in common with others through
inheritance.

     In the other four variables, the test statistic
was significant at the .05 level only when testing
empresas rurais against the other two types, either
together or separately. Owners of empresas rurais
are more likely than owners of minifundios or latifundios to (1) have higher educational levels; (2)
be foreign-born; (3) have other remunerative activities; (4) be multiowners. Caution should be exercised in drawing implications from the national-
origin variable, since the number of foreign-born
that could be discerned in the sample was only 16,
while 11 responses could not be scored.

Land Characteristics

     Only two useful measures of land characteristics
could be derived from the data on the IBRA cards--
the amount of useable land and the value of the land
per hectare. Since both of these variables are of
interval scale, difference-of-means tests were applied
In the useable-land measure, all three property
types have means significantly different from each

other at the .05 level. Empresas rurais have the
highest mean quantity of useable land--201 hectares.
Latifundios, on the average, have only half as much
useable land, with a mean of 101 hectares, while the
mean for minifundios is 8. On the other hand, mean
land values per hectare vary from the high of
Cr$133,762 for minifundios to the low of Cr$110,137
for latifundios. Empresas rurais lie between the
two extremes, with a mean of Cr$130,047. The only
significant difference between these means at the
.05 level is that between minifundios and latifundios. Thus while minifundios have only small
amounts of useable land, the land they do encompass
has a significantly higher mean value than that
occupied by latifundios and is not significantly
different in value from the land held in empresas
rurais.

Production Decisions

Production decisions were treated in three different categories: (1) tenure arrangements; (2)
capital and labor inputs; (3) land use.

Four tenure characteristics were tested. Three
of these are nominal variables and were tested by
Chi-square. In two of these three attributes, tenancy and sharecropping, no significant Chi-square
resulted. On this basis it can be concluded that
none of the property types is more likely than the
others to be worked by tenant farmers or sharecroppers. On the third variable tested by Chi-
square, the use of wage labor, all three types
appear to be different from each other. Empresas
rurais are more likely to use wage laborers than
latifundios, which in turn more commonly employ wage
laborers than latifundios, which in turn more
commonly employ wage laborers than do minifundios.
The fourth variable, percentage of land under the
owner's use, was tested by difference of means. No
significant t-score resulted.

In all, seven interval-scale values were grouped
under the heading of capital and labor inputs.
Each was subjected to difference-of-means tests.
The total number of t-scores derived in this category was twenty-one (seven variables times three
property combinations). Twenty of these t-scores
are significant at the .05 level, demonstrating
a marked difference among the three property types
in labor and capital inputs.

Empresas rurais have mean scores that are significantly higher than the other two types in six
of the variables: (1) the total number of laborers
used; (2) the number of wage laborers; (3) total
capital applied; (4) capital applied per laborer; (5)
capital applied per hectare; (6) technical level.

Minifundios have a mean input of labor per
hectare higher than the means for either of the
other two types. They also have a mean for capital
applied per laborer significantly higher than the
mean for latifundios. In all other tests but one,
although the means for latifundios are significantly
lower than those for empresas rurais, they are
significantly above those for minifundios. The lone
exception is capital applied per hectare, whose
means for latifundios and minifundios are not
significantly different at the .05 level.

In comparison to the other two types, then,
empresas rurais have high inputs, except for labor
input per hectare, in which they are intermediate
between the other two types. Latifundios have
intermediate levels of input in four of the variables, low input in two, and intermediate-low on the
remaining one. Minifundios have high labor input
per hectare, intermediate input of capital per
laborer, intermediate-low input of capital per hectare, and low inputs of the remaining four variables.

The rural land of Bragança Paulista is used
predominantly for producing six basic items: corn,
rice, beans, coffee, cattle, and forest products.
Small amounts of land are devoted to the production
of a wide range of additional crops, none of which
occupies more than 3 per cent of the useable land.
These uses were grouped together under the heading
"Specialty Crops." The area occupied by each of
these seven uses on a given property was divided by
the total useable land on that property and the result multiplied by 100 to yield the percentage of
useable land placed in each use. These property
figures were then added within property classes and
divided by the number of properties within their
class to yield the means that were tested.

The difference-of-means tests seem to indicate
several significant differences among the various
land uses. Empresas rurais, more than the other two
property types, tend to grow coffee and produce
forest products. Minifundios have significantly

higher means than either empresas rurais or latifundios in the percentage of land devoted to beans
and specialty crops.   Latifundios have a higher
mean percentage of land in cattle than either of the
other two property types, but their mean is only
significantly higher than that of empresas rurais.
There is no difference among the property types in
the percentage of land in corn and rice.

Outputs

Two measures of output were tested, gross income per laborer and gross income per hectare.   The
means for latifundios are significantly below the means
for the other two property types in both measures, and
empresas rurais have a higher mean in income per
laborer than minifundios.   Although the minifundio mean
for gross income per hectare is above that for empresas
rurais, there is no statistically significant difference
between these means at the .05 level.

Empresas rurais, then, are more likely to
achieve higher returns per laborer than either of
the other two types, and higher returns per hectare
than latifundios.   Minifundios are likely to have
higher returns both per hectare and per laborer than
latifundios, and returns per hectare that are
approximately equal to those for empresas rurais.

CHARACTERISTICS OF PROPERTY TYPES

Compared to their counterparts, empresas rurais
are more likely to be held by more than one owner
and more likely to have owners who are foreign-born.
Their owners are likely to have higher levels of
education and to pursue other remunerative activities in addition to farming.   Empresas rurais tend
to be larger than minifundios, and their owners tend
to utilize wage laborers, to employ more laborers,
to capitalize these laborers and their properties
more heavily, and to practice higher technical
levels in the operation of their holdings.   In addition, they are more likely to have a greater percentage of their lands devoted to the production of
coffee and forest products.   Empresas rurais tend
to generate greater gross incomes, both in total
and per laborer.

On the other hand, empresas rurais do not
differ significantly from latifundios and

minifundios in other ways that generally have been
held to have operational meaning. They are just as
likely as these other types to have tenants and/or
sharecroppers, to be held in common through inheritance, and to be held by owners who neither reside
upon them nor administer them.

    Minifundios, in comparison to the other types,
are smaller, are operated at lower technical levels,
employ fewer laborers, and apply less capital. But
their intensity of labor input, as measured in
laborers per hectare, is significantly greater than
that of either empresas rurais or latifundios.
Minifundios, in comparison to latifundios, have
higher-value land per unit area, capitalize labor
more heavily, and generate higher gross incomes per
hectare. They are less likely than either empresas
rurais or latifundios to utilize wage labor.

    Many of the characteristics of latifundios can
be inferred from the descriptions above. Latifundios are much like minifundios in the attributes of
their owners, in their intensity of capital input,
and the uses to which their lands are put. They
significantly differ from, and lie between, empresas
rurais and minifundios in size, labor force, total
capital applied, and technical level. Their intensity of labor input, capitalization of labor, and
gross income per hectare are significantly lower
than either of the other two types. Latifundios
tend to occupy land of lower value than minifundios,
and generally have a greater percentage of land devoted to cattle than empresas rurais.

                THE STRATEGIC VARIABLES

    In the preceeding characterizations, care was
taken to avoid assigning cause-and-effect relationships among the variables that seem to differentiate
the property types. The limitations of the data
available militate against the construction of a
precise, definitive model of a healthy farm unit in
the Brazilian context. The data on inputs of labor,
land, and capital are far too gross to permit the
extrapolation of functions that are fully meaningful
for prediction. Nevertheless, some insights may be
gained through the construction of a rudimentary
model that will aid in explaining the differences
between empresas rurais, minifundios, and latifundios in Bragança Paulista.

In describing the results of the statistical
tests, the variables were arranged in four groups:
(1) owner attributes; (2) land characteristics; (3)
production decisions; (4) outputs. Implicit in this
arrangement is a model of the rural productive process.   Owners have a resource (land) under their
control. The kinds of decisions made about the use
of this resource depends upon the nature of the
owner and the amount and/or quality of the land.
These decisions, in turn, lead to outputs that are
dependent upon the wisdom of the decisions.

It is clear that a more elaborate model would
include feedbacks from one category to another. For
example, there are partial results all along the
line that might bring revisions in the original decisions, and the results of a given year are likely
to affect subsequent decisions, It is even possible
to go back to an earlier stage that defines the way
in which people of differing attributes come into
possession of the land. For the present purpose,
however, the simpler model is sufficient.

The statistical tests used indicate that latifundios and minifundios are not significantly different from each other in owner attributes. On the
other hand, empresas rurais are different from both
types in that their owners tend to be more highly
educated, to be foreign-born, and to have other
remunerative activities. In addition, empresas
rurais are likely to have more than one owner. Of
these attributes, only one, educational level, seems
to have operational meaning. Intuitively, it seems
unwise to assign strategic significance to either
multiownership or the fact that the owner's attention is devoted, at least part of the time, to
another activity. In fact, it is more likely that
these features have achieved healthy farm status in
spite of these characteristics. Finally, it was
indicated earlier that the incidence of foreign-born
was too small to permit meaningful statistical in-
ference from Chi-square.

In the two land-resource variables, empresas
rurais are different from latifundios and minifundios only in the quantity of useable land. The
quality of the land, as expressed in per-unit land
value, is approximately the same for empresas rurais
as for the other two types. Of these two resource

characteristics, then, only size appears to bear
any promise as a possible explainer of the differences between the types.

This line of reasoning isolates two strategic
variables, educational level and farm size. The
implications of educational level are obvious, but
what exactly is the impact of size? The role played
by size in property type differentiation is probably
most clearly defined through a comparison of empresas rurais and minifundios in their application of
capital and labor. On a simple fair-share basis,
larger properties would be expected to receive
greater inputs of both these factors. But in addition, small holders undoubtedly find it more difficult to accumulate capital or float credits. Then
too, the capital and labor absorption capacities of
small holdings can be expected to be quite small,
with diminishing or even negative returns being
reached after only meager inputs of these factors.
In Bragança Paulista, minifundios have an average of
0.83 laborers per hectare. There seems little doubt
that this high density indicates disguised unemployment on most such holdings. This notion of disguised unemployment is reinforced by the fact that
while minifundios have high labor densities, their
income densities are smaller than those of empresas
rurais.

The problems of capital and labor, capital being scarce on minifundios and labor being overly
ample, probably affects the choice of commodities to
be produced. Thus coffee cultivation and forestry
are commonly practiced on empresas rurais, but
rarely on minifundios. Both of these activities, as
practiced in Bragança Paulista, require heavy initial inputs of capital, but require heavy labor
input only during short periods of the year. Thus
both are heavy users of capital and ineffecient
absorbers of labor, and neither seems appropriate
for small holders who already find their labor
underemployed.

The composite result of this set of circumstances is low incomes to minifundistas. The low
incomes, in turn, inhibit capital accumulation and
expenditures on such measures of technical level as
seed selection, stock improvement, and control of
soil erosion, insects, and plant and animal
diseases. A significant adjunct to size in

preventing the attainment of higher technical levels
on minifundios is the low level of education and the
generally low levels of expectations and morale
engendered by poverty.

The fact that minifundios do not differ significantly from empresas rurais in land value seems to
support the Brazilian government's disdain for small
holdings. It is not that minifundistas own poor
land, but that they own too little of it to reap
rewards consistent with playing a meaningful role
in Brazilian society and the nation's economy.

If size is the critical factor in developing
the characteristics that differentiate empresas
rurais, it seems only slightly less potent in the
creation of latifundios by use. This third property
type bears a close similarity to minifundios. Minifundios and latifundios are not statistically
different in any of their owner attributes as measured by Chi-square. While their means are significantly different in nine of the nineteen interval
variables, latifundios also differ from empresas
rurais in most of these, and in many lie between
empresas rurais and minifundios.

In Bragança Paulista, latifundios by use average 101 hectares in size, while empresas rurais
are almost twice as large, averaging 201 hectares.
In total capital applied, total laborers, and
technical level, latifundios rank between the other
two types. In addition, little of their land is
devoted to either coffee or forest. Even though
latifundistas devote a greater percentage of their
land to cattle than do minifundistas, the means
for these property types in this variable are not
significantly different. In fact, in all land-use
categories the means of latifundios are adjacent to
minifundios.

The argument that a "latifundio by use" is a
special type of minifundio is hampered somewhat by
the fact that empresas rurais stand at an intermediate position between the two in means on laborers per hectare, gross income per hectare, and land
value per hectare. The fact that lower-value land
is occupied by latifundios could be interpreted to
mean that latifundios actually have a smaller
effective amount of land than that which their
owners have declared to be "useable." If this
interpretation is accurate, then the three property

types should be compared on the basis of their labor
inputs and incomes per unit of _effective_ land rather
than per unit of _useable_ land. On this basis, latifundios are probably more like minifundios than they
are like empresas rurais. The authors realize that
this is a highly speculative and tenuous argument,
but suggest it as a possibility for additional
investigation.

For all these reasons, the reader may decide to
reject size as the strategic factor in differenti-
ating empresas rurais and latifundios. In that
event, the key to the differences between them must
lie either in educational levels or in variables
that cannot be analyzed directly within the context
of the data available to the authors, such as traditional attitudes toward the ownership and use of
land. It is also possible that more highly refined
data could provide more satisfying results.

Subject to all the limitations of the data
available, the following picture is suggested:
Empresas rurais are larger than latifundios and
minifundios and are under control of holders with
higher levels of education. Their larger size pre-
sents the opportunity for greater economic gain
through larger inputs of labor and capital, the
application of higher technical levels of exploitation, and the production of the most rewarding
commodities. Their owners' higher educational level
presumably encourages and permits them to take advantage of this opportunity. Their decision to do
so bears fruit in the form of higher incomes, and
success, in turn, provides incentive for repetition
of these decisions. Even more significant, success
may create a psychological and economic atmosphere
in which innovations are more likely to be intro-
duced and adjustment to changing economic conditions
is more likely to occur.

Smaller properties tend to be held by owners
with low educational levels, and their small size
operates as a deterrent to capital investment, mili-
tates against the efficient use of labor, and
restricts the range of commodities that may be
grown profitably. The low educational level, in
conjunction with small size, inhibits the practice
of higher technical levels. All these conditions
result in low incomes. The resultant poverty re-
inforces the limitations of size and education by
engendering frustration and reduced expectations.

This picture to some extent describes the process that develops the characteristics of minifundios and empresas rurais. It provides less understanding of latifundios by use, especially the larger ones. Certainly low educational levels are characteristic of latifundistas and have the consequences described above, and the smaller latifundios are probably handicapped by small size in the same way minifundios are. It may well be that many properties classified "latifundio by use" are below the size threshold consistent with economic viability. If this is true, IBRA has seriously underestimated this threshold in Bragança Paulista, and possibly in other areas as well.

NOTE

1. The test format and formulae are explained in Hubert M. Blalock, Social Statistics (New York: McGraw-Hill,1960), pp. 172-176.

CHAPTER 7 THE IBRA VIEW OF A RURAL
REALITY: A CASE STUDY
OF BRAGANÇA PAULISTA
MUNICÍPIO

The previous chapters of this book dealt with
the internal logic and functions of the IBRA system,
with why and how it classified a property. This
case study portrays IBRA's view of a rural reality
and attempts to determine the significance of its
classification and tax systems to the properties
themselves and to the município. A serious comparison of IBRA's view of the Bragança rural environment with other existing views is precluded by
the paucity of statistical and descriptive information on the município. Nevertheless, some agricultural census data and a few fragments of
occupance history do tend to corroborate what IBRA
refines from the questionnaires. As for the effect
on the properties themselves: Where do they fall in
the classification system and why, and what do the
resulting classifications and taxes mean to a given
property? Assuming that IBRA can force changes in
individual properties, what will the aggregate
effect be on land agglomeration, which could send a
stream of erstwhile small landholders to the cities,
and on tax collections, whose allocation within the
município could have an impact on Bragança's rural
environment.

WHY BRAGANÇA?

Bragança Paulista's location and resource base
typify what is probably the most critical agricultural environment in Brazil. Despite their depleted
soils, areas such as these, with good transportation
to nearby burgeoning cities, may be Brazil's only
hope for providing urban food supplies. Only close
to urban centers can quantities of foodstuffs be
produced without adding high transportation costs
to the high costs of increasing land productivity.

It is unlikely that in the forseeable future, real
urban income will rise sufficiently to afford the
costs of both high agricultural capitalization and
transportation from distant food sources. IBRA, of
course, is not directly concerned with providing
urban food supplies, but any IBRA-caused changes in
areas such as Bragança Paulista clearly should help
stabilize both the flow and costs of foodstuffs.

    Although Bragança Paulista is readily accessi-
ble to São Paulo, it is in many ways just beyond
the city's zone of functional dominance. The
município is located only forty miles north of the
capital's 6 million inhabitants, along a paved highway (BR 55) that was completed in the early 1960's
between São Paulo and Belo Horizonte. IBRA has
assigned the Bragança physiographic zone, of which
the município is a part, Brazil's fifth highest min-
imal unimproved land value (Cr$81,000). This high
level of assessment clearly reflects the zone's potential urban ties and ignores its existing stagnant
agricultural activity and depleted resource base.
The production of xu-xu (pronounced "shoe-shoe"), a
popular, succulent squashlike vegetable, along the
highway twenty miles north of São Paulo, in Atibaia
município, is an obvious response to the large São
Paulo market. But in the twenty miles between
Atibaia and Bragança Paulista, this type of market
gardening disappears.

    The município's proximity to the second largest
city in the western hemisphere is not at all apparent in its principal administrative and market center, Bragança Paulista, the focus of most of the
activities of the município's 69,152 inhabitants.
Indeed, the hilly site and casual pattern of this
town of 29,452 are more like communities in Minas
Gerais than like neat, taut Paulista towns such as
Atibaia. The Mineiro influence on Bragança has
probably been at least as great as the Paulista
since the early eighteenth century, when Bragança
lay on an important route between São Paulo and the
Minas Gerais gold fields.

    Neither is Bragança's proximity to São Paulo
apparent in its quiet rural landscape, which phys-
ically is reminiscent of North Carolina's Piedmont.
In both places red soils have developed on rolling
to hilly crystalline uplands. In Bragança, however,
these uplands lie at an elevation of 2,500 feet,

1,500 feet higher than in Piedmont. Even their
original vegetation covers were similar: thick
broadleaf forests punctuated by groves of pine (in
Braganca, the southern hemisphere araucária).

During the middle nineteenth century, great
tracts of Bragança's slope forests were replaced by
coffee. But as the center of coffee production
shifted north and west onto the terra roxa soils,
Bragança became an area of marginal production,
marked by old and deteriorating coffee trees on
eroding hillsides. Slowly these have been turned to
the grazing of rachitic cattle or allowed to grow up
in scrub forest (capoeira). Coffee is still produced for cash on some of the larger holdings, but
currently Bragança Paulista, which has long been
known to the people of the state as the zone of
caipira (backwoodsman) agriculture, is dominated by
small holders whose low-input production of such
crops as corn, rice, beans, bananas, citrus fruits,
and cattle tend to provide only subsistence. To
aggravate the situation still further, land fragmentation has been accelerating.

LAND FRAGMENTATION

The federal agricultural census (IBGE[1]) reports
that the number of properties in Bragança Paulista
more than doubled between 1950 and 1960, rising
from 1,801 to 3,694 in a decade that saw no change
in the area of the município (Table 34). The number
of holdings 0-10 hectares in size trebled, so that
by 1960 they made up 65 per cent of the total. For
the same period, there was only a mild increase in
the 10-100 hectare class, and losses in larger-size
categories.

The Department of Statistics of the State of
São Paulo records a total of 6,717 properties in
Bragança Paulista município for 1961 (Table 35),
a figure almost twice IBGE's for 1960. São Paulo
State's figures also show a greater percentage of
very small properties than do IBGE's. In fact, São
Paulo reports 1,264 properties, or 18.8 per cent of
Bragança's total, as less than one hectare in size,
and 73 per cent in the 0-10 hectare class.

By July, 1967, owners of 1,980 properties in
the município had filled out and returned IBRA
questionnaires. From this total 5 per cent of the

TABLE 34

Numbers and Sizes of Properties in
Bragança Paulista, IBGE, 1950 and 1960

size category Ha.	IBGE 1950			IBGE 1960		
	number	per cent	area in hectares	number	per cent	area in hectares
0-10	785	43.5	4,005	2,411	65.4	11,260
10-100	848	47.2	26,779	1,144	31.0	34,235
100-1,000	164	9.1	43,201	138	3.8	35,500
1,000-10,000	4	.2	7,481	1	negl.	1,283
10,000+	0	0	0	0	0	0
Total	1,801	100.0	81,466	3,694	100.0	82,278

TABLE 35

Numbers and Sizes of Properties in Bragança Paulista,
Department of Statistics, State of São Paulo, 1961

size category in hectares	number	per cent	number	per cent
less than 1.0	1,264	18.8		
1.0-1.9	854	12.7		
2.0-2.9	688	10.5		
3.0-3.9	507	7.5		
4.0-4.9	482	7.1	4,952	73.8
5.0-9.9	1,157	17.2		
10-100			1,585	23.4
100-1,000			177	2.8
1,000-10,000			3	negl.
10,000+			0	0
Total			6,717	100.0

TABLE 36

Number and Classification of Bragança Properties Based
on IBRA Questionnaires Returned by the End of 1966:
Bragança Total and an Analysis Sample

Property Class	Actual IBRA Count		Sample Taken for Analysis	
	No.	%	No.	% of IBRA Count
Minifundio	1,628	82.3	85	5.2
Empresa Rural	59	3.0	59	100.0
Latifundio	293	14.7	70	23.8

minifundios and 24 per cent of the latifundios,
selected at random, and all the empresas rurais were
chosen to form a 214-property sample (Table 36).
The properties in this sample are categorized by
size in Table 37. Were all 1,980 properties tabu-
lated by size, one could expect the smaller-size
classes in Table 37 to contain greater percentages
of the total number of properties, since propor-
tionately more minifundios and small latifundios by
use would be included. Even in its present form,
however, Table 37 approximates São Paulo's percentages in some of the very small categories.

It is difficult to determine just how close any
of these sets of figures comes to the actual number
of holdings in the município. Each of the three
sets of figures calls into question the other two.
The truth of the matter may be: (1) that the IBGE
figures are rational estimates; (2) that São Paulo's
figures count sharecroppers and tenants as landholders; (3) that IBRA's tabulation probably represents only about two-thirds of the actual number of
Bragança properties. This last possibility is based
on the fact that when the area of each of the three
classes of properties in the sample is projected to
100 per cent and the results added, the total area
of all properties in Bragança is about 57 per cent
of the total area of the município. Assuming 15 per
cent of the município area to be nonfarm, then the
1,980 farms make up about two-thirds of the remaining area, and thus two-thirds of the total number of
farms.

IBRA-CLASSIFIED BRAGANÇA RURAL PROPERTIES

By now the reader knows that small size alone
does not make an IBRA minifundio. In this "zone
of the caipira," however, small size and inefficien-
cy go hand in hand to force 82 per cent of the IBRA-
registered properties (1,628 of 1,980) into the
minifundio category (Table 36). Only 15 per cent
(293) are latifundios, and a pitiful 3 per cent (59)
are empresas rurais. Bragança truly is a "zone of
the caipira," for in the whole of São Paulo State
only 60 per cent of rural properties are
minifundios.

TABLE 37

Size Categories Within the IBRA Classification for the Sample of 214 Bragança Properties.

Areal Size Category	Minifundios				Empresas Rurais				Latifundios			
	No.	%	No.	%	No.	%	No.	%	No.	%	No.	%
0-1.0	6	7.1			–				–			
1.0-1.9	12	14.1			–				–			
2.0-2.9	13	15.3			–				–			
3.0-3.9	4	4.8	61	72.0	–				–			
4.0-4.9	8	9.4			–				–			
5.0-9.9	18	21.3			1	1.9	1	1.9	–			
10-100			24	28.0			24	40.5				
100-1,000			–				34	57.6			48	68.7
1,000-10,000			–				–				22	31.3
10,000+			–				–				–	
Total			85	100.0			59	100.0			70	100.0

Areal Category	All Properties in Sample			
	No.	%	No.	%
0-1.0	6	2.8		
1.0-1.9	12	5.6		
2.0-2.9	13	6.1		
3.0-3.9	4	4.8	62	29.0
4.0-4.9	8	9.4		
5.0-9.9	18	21.3		
10-100			96	44.8
100-1,000			56	26.2
1,000-10,000			–	
10,000+			–	
Total			214	100.0

Bragança Minifundios

Lack of size in modulos is the whole story.
These properties are disqualified from empresa rural
status at IBRA's first level of differentiation,
because not one can support a family of four adults
at IBRA-specified levels (see Chapter 2). And aside
from IBRA's emphasis on modulos, minifundios tend to
be extremely small. In the sample, they range in
area from 0.2 to 50.0 hectares, with a mean size of
9.3 hectares.[2]

It is also interesting to note the poverty of
minifundios in economic and social status. While
their mean CEY is only slightly better than that of
latifundios (Table 39), their mean CSC is much worse
(Table 40). Twelve minifundios (20 per cent) pass
IBRA's CEY test and 50 (85 per cent) pass the CSC
test (Figure 11), but not one property passes both.
So even if they were at least one modulo in size,
all would still be latifundios by use and not empresas rurais.

Minifundios have better market access than
latifundios, but poorer access than empresas (Table
41). Thus their mean CL lies between the means of
the other two groups.

Bragança Latifundios

Slightly more than 14 per cent of Bragança's
properties (293 of 1,980) are classified by IBRA as
latifundios. From the value of the four coefficients shown in Figure 12, it is apparent that economic conditions, not size or social conditions, are
responsible for the majority of latifundio classifications.

Surprisingly, the mean CD for latifundios is
lower than the mean for empresas rurais (Table 38).
The mean latifundio in the sample had 102.2 hectares,
while the mean empresa contains 214.7. Bragança's
largest latifundio has 479 hectares; its largest
empresa, 758. Obviously, for IBRA, large size alone
does not make a latifundio.

Only three of the properties that escaped lati-
fundio-by-size and minifundio status meet IBRA's
economic norms--that is, have CEY's below 1.3 (Table
39 and arrows on Figure 12). Ironically, one of
these economically sound three fails the social

TABLE 38

Distribution of Coefficients of Dimension
Within the 214-Property Bragança Sample

CD	Minifundios No.	%	Empresas Rurais No.	%	Latifundios No.	%	Total No.	%
1.0	77	90.6	6	10.2	7	10.0	90	42.3
1.1	2	2.4	2	3.4			4	1.8
1.2			1	1.7	1	1.4	2	.9
1.3					3	4.3	3	1.4
1.4					1	1.4	1	.4
1.5	6	7.0	37	62.7	49	70.0	92	43.2
1.6								
1.7			2	3.4			2	.9
1.8								
1.9								
2.0			8	13.5	6	8.7	14	6.5
2.5					1	1.4	1	.4
3.0			1	1.7	1	1.4	2	.9
3.5								
4.0			2	3.4			2	.9
4.5								
Total	85	100.0	59	100.0	70	100.0	214	100.0
Means	$\bar{x} = 1.03$		$\bar{x} = 1.61$		$\bar{x} = 1.55$		$\bar{x} = 1.37$	

TABLE 39

Distribution of Coefficients of Economic Yield
Within the 214-Property Bragança Sample

CEY	Minifundios No.	%	Empresas Rurais No.	%	Latifundios No.	%	Total No.	%
0.4			2	3.4			2	.9
0.5			4	6.8			4	1.9
0.6	1	1.2	2	3.4			3	1.4
0.7	1	1.2	1	1.7			2	.9
0.8			4	6.8			4	1.9
0.9	3	3.5	6	10.2			9	4.2
1.0	1	1.2	11	18.6			12	5.7
1.1	3	3.5	14	23.7			17	7.9
1.2	3	3.5	15	25.4	3	4.2	21	9.8
1.3	8	9.4			12	17.2	20	9.3
1.4	19	22.3			26	37.1	45	21.0
1.5	46	54.2			29	41.5	75	35.1
Total	85	100.0	59	100.0	70	100.0	214	100.0
Means	$\bar{x} = 1.38$		$\bar{x} = .977$		$\bar{x} = 1.41$		$\bar{x} = 1.28$	

TABLE 40

Distribution of the Coefficients of Social Conditions
Within the 214-Property Bragança Sample

CSC	Minifundios No.	%	Empresas Rurais No.	%	Latifundios No.	%	Total No.	%
0.3	1	1.2	–		2	2.8	3	1.4
0.4	23	27.0	5	8.5	10	14.3	38	17.8
0.5	8	9.4	10	16.9	12	17.2	30	14.0
0.6	3	3.5	15	25.4	10	14.3	28	13.0
0.7	9	10.6	15	25.4	11	15.7	35	16.4
0.8	3	3.5	5	8.5	6	8.6	14	6.5
0.9	3	3.5	5	8.5	1	1.4	9	4.2
1.0	–		4	6.8	4	5.7	8	3.7
1.1	2	2.4			3	4.3	5	2.3
1.2	11	12.9			2	2.8	13	6.1
1.3	10	11.8			3	4.3	13	6.1
1.4	10	11.8			6	8.6	16	7.5
1.5	1	1.2			–	–	1	.5
1.6	1	1.2			–	–	1	.5
Total	85	100.0	59	100.0	70	100.0	214	100.0
Means	$\bar{x}$ = .849		$\bar{x}$ = .644		$\bar{x}$ = .742		$\bar{x}$ = .762	

TABLE 41

Distribution of the Coefficients of Location
Within the 214-Property Bragança Sample

CL	Minifundios No.	%	Empresas Rurais No.	%	Latifundios No.	%	Total No.	%
1.0	–							
1.1	–							
1.2	1	1.2			5	7.1	6	2.8
1.3	48	56.5	24	40.6	44	62.9	116	54.2
1.4	36	42.3	35	59.4	21	30.0	92	43.0
1.5	–	–	–	–	–	–	–	–
Total	85	100.0	59	100.0	70	100.0	214	100.0
Means	$\bar{x}$ = 1.32		$\bar{x}$ = 1.35		$\bar{x}$ = 1.29		$\bar{x}$ = 1.34	

FIGURE 11

Tax Rates and Component Coefficients
for Bragança Paulista Minifundios

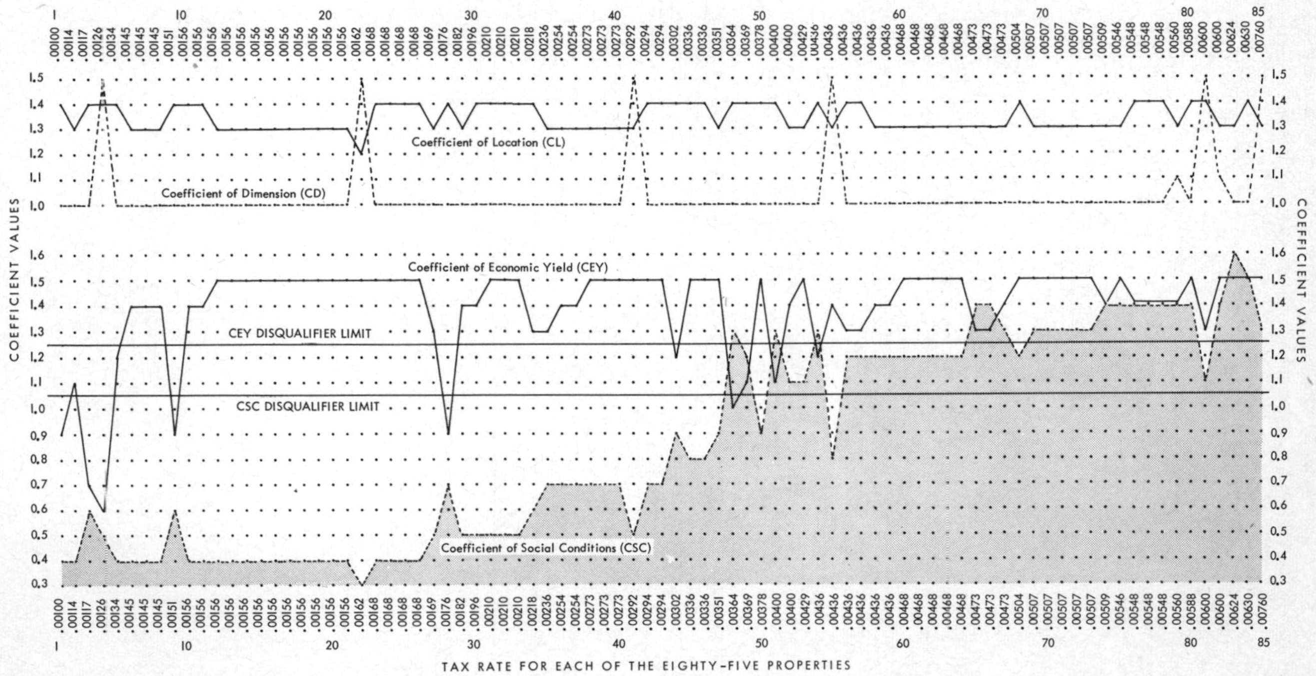

(CSC) test. The other two pass both the CSC and CEY
hurdles, only to be classed as latifundios by use
because their crop yields (reflected in the AYF component of the CEY) are too low. As Table 39 indicates, the mean CEY for latifundios is high at 1.4.

Fifty-six of Bragança's latifundios (80 per
cent) meet IBRA's social standards by having CSC's
below 1.1. They are classified as latifundios by
use on the basis of their CEY's or AYF's,but their
social conditions' are moderately good. They have a
mean CSC of 0.7, well below that for minifundios
(Table 40).

Latifundios have the worst access to market of
any of the types. Their mean CL of 1.29 is lowest
among the three groups (Table 41).

Bragança Empresas Rurais

The "zone of the caipira" is inhospitable to
empresas rurais. Only 3 per cent of Bragança's
holdings (59 of 1,980) meet all of IBRA's standards
of what a rural property in this urban-proximal
physiographic zone should be.

The pattern of CD's for empresas (Figure 13) is
similar to that for latifundios (Figure 12), but
since the level of this coefficient is generally
higher for an empresa, the mean CD for all empresas
is 1.61, as opposed to 1.55 for latifundios (Table
38). As noted previously, empresas average more
than twice the hectarage of latifundios. This means
that many owners who capitalize their land, use it
fully, and produce well (reflected in the IF, UF,
and AYF) do so on a rather large scale in IBRA terms.
For example, each of the eleven empresas with a CD
of 2.0 or more is capable of supporting at least
forty-four adults at IBRA levels.

Empresas are weakest in economic conditions.
Fifteen, or fully one-quarter of the total, have
CEY's of 1.2 (Table 39) and thus lie just below the
disqualifying level on IBRA's economic test.

As a group, empresas have excellent social conditions. The mean is at 0.6, well below the means
for minifundios and latifundios (Table 40), and few
empresas even come close to the 1.1 disqualifying
limit.

FIGURE 12

Tax Rates and Component Coefficients
for Bragança Paulista Latifundios

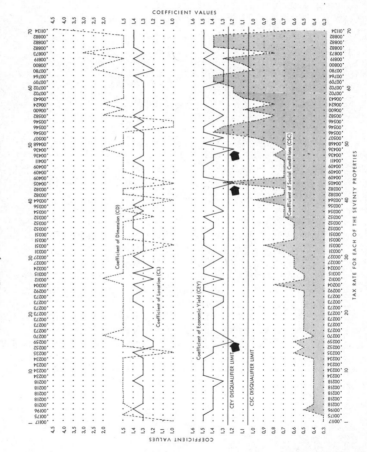

FIGURE 13

Tax Rates and Component Coefficients for Bragança Paulista Empresas Rurais

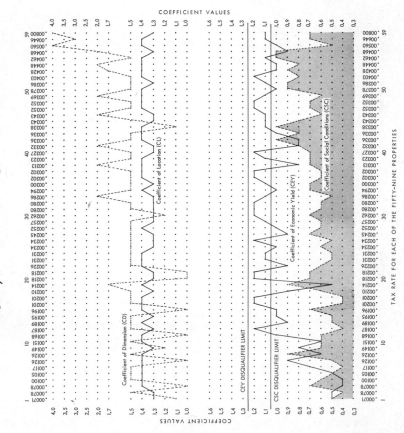

Empresas' mean CL is 1.35 (Table 41), higher
than both munifundios and latifundios. Whether
sound rural entrepreneurs seek out good locations or
good locations attract entrepreneurs and capital is
difficult to say. At any rate, empresas have
potentially higher taxes because of their good
access to market.

IBRA TAXES ON BRAGANÇA RURAL PROPERTIES

As we have seen, IBRA determines the tax rate
for a property by multiplying its four coefficients
times a constant:
CD x CEY x CSC x CL x .002=Rural Land Tax Rate

Latifundios have the highest tax rate in
Bragança becouse of their high CD's and very high
(poor) CEY's (Table 42). The resulting mean tax
rate for the group, calculated by multiplying the
mean of each coefficient, is .0042. Figure 14
shows the dispersion of rates from that mean and
provides a graphic illustration of why the mean tax
rate for latifundios is statistically significantly
different from the means for minifundios and
empresas rurais.

Applying the "t" test to the difference between
the mean tax rates for latifundios and minifundios
indicates that this difference (shown by dashed
lines on Figure 14) is significant at the .01 level.
This means that there is less than one chance in 100
that a random selection of latifundio and minifundio
tax rates, given the dispersions shown on Figure 14,
would yield the same difference between these two
means. Between latifundios and empresas rurais, the
difference is even more significant. The "t" test
puts it at the .001 level. On the basis of tax rates
latifundios are clearly set apart from minifundios and
empresas rurais.

The minifundios' expectedly low CD is compensated by a high CEY and a very high CSC, to yield a
mean tax rate of .0032 (Table 42). The "t" test
indicates that the means and their accompanying
dispersals shown in Figure 14 are not significantly
different from those of the empresas rurais.

Despite extremes in two coefficients, this
group of holdings has the lowest mean tax rate in
Bragança. Very low (good) CEY and CSC levels
balance off very high CD and CL values to produce
a mean tax rate of .0027. According to the "t"

TABLE 42

Means for Each of the Four Coefficients and Resulting Mean Tax Rates for the Three Property Groups in the Bragança Sample

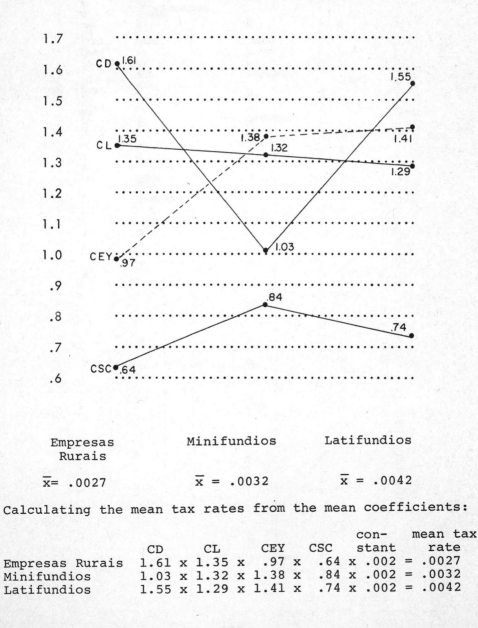

	Empresas Rurais	Minifundios	Latifundios
	$\overline{x}= .0027$	$\overline{x} = .0032$	$\overline{x} = .0042$

Calculating the mean tax rates from the mean coefficients:

	CD	CL	CEY	CSC	con-stant	mean tax rate
Empresas Rurais	1.61 x	1.35 x	.97 x	.64 x	.002 =	.0027
Minifundios	1.03 x	1.32 x	1.38 x	.84 x	.002 =	.0032
Latifundios	1.55 x	1.29 x	1.41 x	.74 x	.002 =	.0042

FIGURE 14

Tax Rate Distributions for Bragança Paulista Empresas Rurais,
Minifundios, and Latifundios

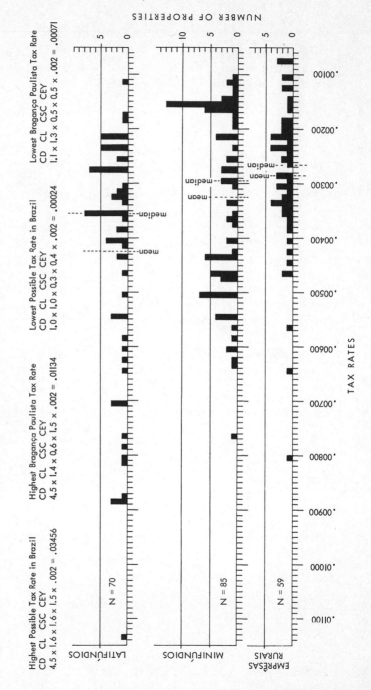

test, this mean is <u>not</u> significantly different from
the minifundio mean. This is because many empresas
and minifundios have similar tax rates (Figure 14).

That the difference between mean tax rates of
0.42 per cent on the one hand, and 0.27 per cent and
0.32 per cent on the other, is "significant" statistically surely says something about the reality
to which IBRA's system is applied. It even suggests
something of IBRA's philosophy or bias. But in more
practical terms, these infinitesimal rates themselves can hardly yield a significant tax unless the
land values by which they are multiplied are of an
entirely different order of magnitude than they are.

OPERATIONAL LAND VALUES AND THE RURAL LAND TAX

Operational land values are the values used by
IBRA to calculate the Rural Land Tax. If the owner
declares no unimproved land value for his property,
it is set by IBRA at the minimum (Cr$81,000,
U.S.$40.50, in Bragança Paulista physiographic zone).
If the owner declares his value to be below the
minimum, IBRA raises it. Otherwise his assessment
of his property's unimproved land value is accepted
for the calculations. In Bragança these values
are very low, and, surprisingly, do not vary radi-
cally per hectare among the three property groups
(Table 43). The average value of an empresa is
Cr$30.7 million (U.S.$15,350), and its mean area is
214.7 hectares, yielding a mean value per hectare
of Cr$143,000, or U.S.$71.50 (about U.S.$28.75 per
acre).[3] The mean tax per hectare is Cr$500
U.S.$0.25), or about ten cents an acre. Thus the
empresa tax in Bragança is one-seventeenth the 1966
U.S. average rural land tax of $1.74 per acre.[4]
For a latifundio, the mean value is Cr$10.8 million
(U.S.$5,400); mean size is 102.2 hectares; mean
value per hectare is Cr$106,000 (U.S.$53.00); mean
tax per hectare Cr$450 (U.S.$0.23), or about nine
cents an acre. For minifundios the mean value is
Cr$1.2 million (U.S.$550); mean size 9.3 hectares;
mean value per hectare Cr$126,000 (U.S.$63.00),
actually larger than the value for the average latifundio; mean tax per hectare Cr$460 (U.S.$0.23)--
nine cents per acre as for latifundios.

OPERATIONAL AND MINIMAL LAND VALUES

The low operational land values may be a function of the low minimum land value. IBRA's minimum Cr$81,000 (U.S.$40.50) per hectare is only U.S.$16.25 per acre. From a comparison of IBRA-set minima with declared land values, it appears that between one-third and one-half of all properties fall into one of the following categories: either the owner declares no value at all or declares below the minimum, so IBRA sets the value at the Cr$81,000 level, or the owner declares just above the minimum, perhaps knowing about the Cr$81,000 figure and fearing to declare below it out of ignorance of what this might mean in the complicated IBRA classification system.

Since so many properties are at or near the minimum, it is a bit surprising that the differences between minimum and operational land values are as great as they are. The ratio is lowest for latifundios at 1 to 1.31; minifundios have a 1 to 1.56 and empresas a 1 to 1.75 ratio (Table 43). In the aggregate, owners of empresas set their property values at one and three-quarters of the minimum. This high ratio, however, is really the product of just fourteen properties whose values are declared at from 2.0 to 9.9 times the minimum (Table 44). Most empresistas declare either just above or just below the minimum, or in some cases not at all, so that their ratios in Table 44 lie at or just above the 1.0 level.

A quick inspection of data for nonempresas shows that fewer owners declared property values, so many more latifundios and minifundios than empresas have a 1 to 1 operational/minimal land-value ratio. And the higher ratios are not so great as those for empresas. The highest positive ratio for a latifundio is a rare 4.3 to 1, based on a declaration of Cr$56,000,000 against a minimum of Cr$13,000,000. For the minifundio group, the highest ratio was 7 to 1, from a declared value of Cr$18,000,000 over a minimum of Cr$2,500,000.

PROPERTY EARNINGS AND THE RURAL LAND TAX

By any measure, the tax burden on all properties is light. Fifty-one of the fifty-nine empresas

TABLE 43

Value and Tax Comparisons of Properties in the Bragança Paulista Sample

	Mean Hectares Per Property	Acres	Average Operational Value Per Hectare		Per Acre	Average Tax Per Hectare		Per Acre
			Cr$	US$	US$	Cr$	US$	US$
Minifundios	9.3	22.9	126,000	63.00	25.20	460	.23	.09
IBRA minimum			81,000	40.50	16.25			
Empresas Rurais	214.7	530.3	143,000	71.50	28.75	500	.25	.10
IBRA minimum			81,000	40.50	16.25			
Latifundios	102.2	252.4	106,000	53.00	21.20	450	.23	.09
IBRA minimum			81,000	40.50	16.25			

	Average Operational Value Per Property		Operational/Minimal Value Ratio	Average Tax Per Property		Mean Tax Rate On Unimproved Value
	Cr$	US$		Cr$	US$	
Minifundios	1,183,000	550	1 : 1.56	4,300	2.15	.0032
IBRA minimum	753,000	376				
Empresas Rurais	30,735,000	15,350	1 : 1.75	107,000	53.50	.0027
IBRA minimum	17,391,000	8,695				
Latifundios	10,824,000	5,400	1 : 1.31	46,000	23.00	.0042
IBRA minimum	8,278,000	4,139				

(N=214: Minifundios=85; Empresas Rurais=59; Latifundios=70)

TABLE 44

Ratio of Operational Unimproved Land Values to
Minimum Unimproved Land Values for 59 Empresas Rurais

Ratio (Operational Divided By Minimum Values)	Number of Properties
1.0 even	12
1.0+	20
1.1	2
1.2	5
1.3	2
1.4	1
1.5	1
1.6	2
2.0	1
2.1	1
2.3	1
2.4	1
2.5	2
3.0	1
3.5	1
4.0	1
4.5	1
5.2	2
5.9	1
9.9	1
$\bar{x} = 1.75$	59

reported sales of produce in the year 1966, which
averaged out to a gross income of more than Cr$18
million (U.S.$9,112) per property (Table 45). The
Rural Land Tax per holding, however, is only Cr$107,
000 (U.S.$53.50), yielding a gross-income/tax ratio
of 170 to 1, or a tax on gross income of 0.6 per
cent. There is absolutely no way of knowing how
much of this gross income is net income, but if we
assume that net income is only 75 per cent of gross
income, this amounts to U.S.$6,750 annually per
empresa. Taxes of U.S.$53.50, then, are 0.8 per cent
of net income, a figure hardly comparable to 1966
U.S. farm real estate taxes of 9.3 per cent of net
farm income.[5] In comparison, the empresas' tax
burden is extremely light.

     The tax burden is even lighter for minifundios,
forty-four of which reported gross incomes averaging
Cr$1.3 million (U.S.$660) in 1966. Assuming again
that net income is 75 per cent of gross, the average
net income of these minifundios is U.S.$487. If a
minifundio supports four persons, the per-capita
income is U.S.$122, or roughly one-half Brazil's
per-capita income. The tax of Cr$4,300 (U.S.$2.15)
per minifundio is low in comparison to earnings, the
ratio being 230 to 1, or a tax of 0.4 per cent on
net income. But minifundios cannot really be dealt
with in this cold, mathematical manner. Too many
are too small and their incomes not only too low,
but also very erratic. Any minor natural or economic change threatens the very life of the minifundio and its occupants. Virtually all minifundistas are exempt from payment of taxes. Without this
exemption, the tax would do more than threaten. It
would probably push the owner into rural-laborer
status (which he may already be part of the time)
or drive him and his family into the city, thus
increasing the burden not only on them but also on
the remaining rural food producers who must now feed
more nonproducers.

     Latifundios have a gross income per property
of Cr$2.3 million (U.S.$1,150), and an estimated net
income of U.S.$860. The mean tax of Cr$46,000
(U.S.$23.00) gives a net-income/tax ratio of 37 to
1. This is a burden of 2.7 per cent on net income,
less than one-third the 1966 U.S. percentage of 9.3.
Low productivity is the key to a poor income/tax
ratio. To increase taxes here might force money to
flow into these properties from, say, the urban-
industrial sector. Yet virtually all of these

TABLE 45

Ratio of Property Gross Incomes to Rural Land Tax for Bragança
Paulista Sample of 214 Holdings: 59 Empresas Rurais, 70 Latifundios
and 85 Minifundios[a]

	Empresas Rurais		Latifundios		Minifundios	
	Cr$	US$	Cr$	US$	Cr$	US$
Total Gross Income	929,439,000	464,720.00	103,703,000	51,851.00	44,898,000	22,449.00
Mean Gross Income Per Property	18,224,294	9,112.00	2,304,511	1,150.00	1,320,529	660.00
Mean Tax Per Property	107,000	53.50	46,000	23.00	4,300	2.15
Ratio of Gross Income to Tax	170 to 1		50 to 1		308 to 1	
Tax as Percent of Gross Income	.06%		2.0%		0.3%	

a Fifty-one of the 59 empresas rurais reported sales in 1966; so did 45 of the 70 latifundios and 34 of the 85 minifundios.

TABLE 46

Bragança Paulista Totals

(Data for each of the three property groups in the sample projected to 100 per cent)[a]

Area	Hectares	Per Cent	Acres
Empresas rurais	12,668.4	21.2	31,291
Minifundios	16,146.7	27.5	39,882
Latifundios	30,052.2	51.3	74,229
Totals	58,867.3	100.0	145,402

Operational Land Value	CR$	Per Cent	US$
Empresas rurais	1,813,356,000	26.2	906,000
Minifundios	1,931,289,000	27.9	966,000
Latifundios	3,182,163,000	45.9	1,591,000
Totals	6,926,809,000	100.0	3,463,000

Total Tax Assessed			
Empresas rurais	6,267,293	30.8	3,133
Minifundios	7,084,032	34.6	3,542
Latifundios	7,098,420	34.6	3,549
Totals	20,449,745	100.0	10,224

Total Tax Owed			
Empresas rurais	6,267,293	34.0	3,133
Minifundios	5,107,200	27.6	2,553
Latifundios	7,087,080	38.4	3,543
Totals	18,461,573	100.0	9,229

a For empresas rurais: 59=100.0%, so 59 x 1.0 = 100.0% of empresas rurais in Bragança. Minifundios: 85=5.2%, so 85 x 19.2 = 100.0% of Bragança minifundios. Latifundios: 70=23.8%, so 70 x 4.2 = 100.0% of Bragança Paulista latifundios.

holdings are latifundios by use--that is, just
slightly bloated minifundios. They are not the
great tracts of the underused and unused lands owned
by urban industrialists or rich dilletantes who
might have the money to invest.

SIGNIFICANCE OF THE TAX TO BRAGANÇA PAULISTA

What this all means to Bragança Paulista município is a total tax assessment of Cr$20 million
(U.S.$10,000) annually, assessed about equally on
the three property groups (Table 46). But actual
tax owed is another matter. Fifty-one minifundios
are exempt from the tax because they contain twenty
or fewer hectares occupied by one family that owns
no other properties. One latifundio and, surprisingly, three empresas are also exempt for the same
reasons. The total potential tax collection for
Bragança thus falls to Cr$18.4 million, or
U.S.$9,200. What could a município possibly do with
this microcosmic bit of capital? Consider for a
moment that if each of the 1,980 properties in the
município were eligible for a loan and made application for one, they would receive U.S.$4.65 each.
By comparison, the U.S. 1966 average rural land tax
of $1.74 per acre times the total number of acres
in Bragança properties (58,867.3 hectares or 145,402
acres) yields a potential tax return to the
município of U.S.$252,997. Bragança Paulista is
trapped in a cycle of very low productivity, which
manifests itself in very low land values and a very
low Rural Land Tax collection.

NOTES

1. Instituto Brasileiro de Geografia e
Estatística, the Brazilian equivalent of the United
States Bureau of the Census.

2. The reader may notice a difference between
these means and those found in Chapter 6. The
difference is because the means in Chapter 6 were
computed from 186 cases, whereas those for Chapter
7 were computed from 214 cases.

3. One hectare equals 2.47 acres, and in 1966
a dollar equaled 2,000 cruzeiros.

4. U.S. Department of Agriculture, Economic
Research Service, Farm Real Estate Taxes, ERS 3013-68(9)
(December 1968).

5. Ibid.

CHAPTER REFORM, COMPROMISE, AND
PRIORITY

Brazil's attempt at agrarian reform is best
understood as a compromise between a complete and
immediate overhaul of the rural sector of the economy and the exigencies of Brazilian reality. Although it seeks to mount an integrated assault on
all facets of the nation's rural ills, IBRA's reform
is seriously constrained by limited resources of
capital, by the huge area over which these resources
must be spread, and by the sociopolitical realities
of the country. The design of the complex classification and taxation systems intended to effect progress in all aspects of rural life is conditioned by
these constraints, and it is in compromise with them
that the greatest strengths and foremost short-
comings of these systems are found. Whether the systems succeed or fail in realizing their goals
depends upon the degree to which the advantages they
gain through compromise can be strengthened and the
weaknesses overcome.

Brazil's new agrarian reform contains three
kinds of compromise: (1) wholly within the Statute;
(2) in the design of the two instrument-systems
(classification and taxation); (3) in the application of these systems. The Statute recognizes that
large holdings, both private and corporate, provide
essential foreign exchange to the economy, so it
makes no attempt to force all properties into the
family-farm mold. And while the Statute places a
heavy value upon the development of an agrarian
middle-class, it recognizes that tenancy, sharecropping, and the wide use of wage labor will per-
sist for a long time to come. As a consequence, the
classificaiton and tax systems are designed to provide a mechanism to reduce the incidence of these
practices in the long run. In addition, the Statute
makes an attempt to avoid levying taxes that are so
high as to drive excessively large numbers of people
from the land.

The design of the systems is geared to incomplete knowledge of farm data. To avoid expensive land-capability analyses, they use information from sample studies as a basis for assumptions about potential production, which are projected to the myriad holdings in Brazil. Since it is almost impossible to collect such highly sophisticated data as out-of-pocket costs, depreciation, labor costs, and the like in Brazil, these are either subsumed under the data that can be collected or are postulated from general economic concepts or prejudices regarding what they should be.

Parts of the systems are designed to permit traditional rural institutions to escape their effect or to be changed gradually. Such compromise is in recognition of the most significant political reality currently facing Brazilian agrarian reform: the delicate balance between traditional, moribund landholders who fight change and dynamic industrial entrepreneurs who demand ordered change. The reform seeks to stimulate rapid change where possible, while holding to a low level destructive opposition from traditional landholders. A case in point is the way in which the Coefficient of Dimension is calculated: multiowned properties, most likely to be large, traditional holdings, appear to be favored by the alternate methods of determining this coefficient.

The most noteworthy compromise made in the application of the classification system is in the determination of priority areas. In these areas, the full force of available resources can be brought to bear upon reform of the decision-making base and agricultural development. The concomitant of this compromise, of course, is reliance on voluntary change in nonpriority areas.

It is clear that each of these compromises serves a useful purpose. Nevertheless, efforts can be made to mitigate the disadvantages incurred in making them. Knowledge about rural holdings can be improved. The proliferation of family farms can be accelerated. Both these goals can be served by finding a way to speed the subdivision of the nonessential large farms in the higher modulo ranges that do not exceed the upper limit of 600 modulos. There is little doubt that many such large holdings are not effective foreign-exchange earners, yet are protected by the umbrella designed to shield those

that are. And land taxes can be raised. It seems
inconceivable that the current level of land taxes
even remotely approaches the critical limit. The
tax constant, .002, could be increased to five times
its present value (to .01) without accelerating the
rural exodus already under way.

The traditional landholder's ability to abort
reform is real, but concessions to **this** group should
not be built into the system on a long-term basis.
Mechanisms should be incorporated to permit a
tightening of economic and social controls as this
group diminishes in size and influence. Above all,
existing loopholes related to the calculation of the
modulo should be closed, to preclude a "paper"
dispersion of property ownership that will not
result in real economic gains for both the rural
sector of the economy and the nation as a whole.

The notion of compromise and priority should be
extended to the components of the system themselves--
specifically to the Coefficient of Social Conditions
and its application. It is possible that an attempt
to enforce investment in social justice in the short
run would divert capital from directly productive
agricultural uses. If this is true, then farm
productivity would fall short of its potential and
the capital available for continued investment in
social conditions would be reduced. Thus, diversion
of capital from directly productive uses might
well abort attempts at economic improvement in the
short run and retard both economic and social
improvement in the long run.

Greater stress should be placed upon the two
components of the Coefficient of Economic Conditions:
the Utilization Factor (UF) and the Agricultural
Yields Factor (AYF). Recall that the UF is the
amount of land used expressed as a percentage of
land that is deemed useable. The AYF is a measure
of crop and/or livestock yields per unit of land.
If improvements occur here, commodity availabilities
will necessarily increase. At the same time, improvements in these measures imply increased input
of capital and increased incomes, conditions expressed in other components of the CEY, the Investment Factor (IF) and the Economic Yields Factor
(EYF). Simplicity of application is yet another
important benefit of stressing the UF and the AYF.

In addition to the extension of compromise and priority suggested above, the government must expand its involvement in the application of the systems at the local levels. It must first see to it that the classification and taxation systems are understood by the people who are expected to make the changes. And then the government must be in a position to verify whether alterations have in fact been made. To implement local involvement, Brazil might create a corps of rural agricultural agents operating at the município or physiographic-zone level. Such agents would interpret the classification and tax system in ways that are meaningful to those who make decisions about the land. Equipped with aerial-photographic coverage of their regions, they would be in a position to check on the UF and AYF. At the same time a corps of such agents would form the basis for a crop-forecasting network, a much-needed but poorly developed function in Brazil today.

Brazil's new agrarian reform is an attempt to transform the nation's rural life. The political, economic, and social realities of the country have made necessary compromise and the assignment of priorities, which can be extended further. Compromise can be extended by deferring application of the CSC. Priority can be extended to the CEY and to two of its components, the AYF and UF, and to the development of a widespread corps of federal agricultural agents charged with encouraging, forcing, and/or aiding change at the local level.

APPENDIXES

APPENDIX A

The Land Inventory Questionnaire
(Translated from the Portuguese)

BRAZILIAN AGRARIAN REFORM INSTITUTE

RURAL PROPERTY DECLARATION

ON FILLING OUT THIS QUESTIONNAIRE, WHICH IS YOUR DECLARATION OF RURAL PROPERTY, REMEMBER:

1) The LAND STATUTE directs that IBRA, in order to correct deficiencies in the national agrarian structure, begin by taking an Inventory of Rural Properties to obtain a picture of rural conditions predominating in the various zones of each state.

2) To this end IBRA institutes the WEEK OF THE LAND during which you will be able to make your DECLARATION OF RURAL PROPERTY (Article 49, Sections 2 and 3, Law No. 4504, 11-30-1964 - ESTATUTO DA TERRA) filling out this Declaration and the indicated Annexes with help, if necessary, from the volunteers of the County Inventory Unit.

3) The Declaration and Annexes will be sold in duplicate (one for your own records) at the price printed on each.

4) Information given should be as accurate as possible since for the development of programs to aid the farmer, rancher or agriculturist in general an exact picture of the Brazilian agricultural situation is indispensable and this can only be obtained through a minute census of the characteristics and conditions on each rural property in each county in the country.

5) Some of the questions on the Declaration may not pertain to your property. You are not obliged then to answer all questions; but when the number of correct responses is large this is evidence of your understanding and interest in the development of the rural property you possess.

6) The Inventory of Rural Property finally seeks to orient the many Federal, State and County agencies so that they may better allocate their resources - coming from taxes - to the promotion of progress and prestige of rural people.

7) If you are in legitimate possession of the land but are without legal documentation do not fail to fill out the Declaration because it will indicate to IBRA the necessity of taking measures to expedite the Título de Posse (Article 11, Law No. 4504, 11-30-1964).

8) The Rural Land Tax (Imposto Territorial Rural or ITR) will be calculated from the data you give on the value of your land and the ways in which it is used and improved. Correct information will be to your benefit in the calculation of the ITR.

9) Upon delivering your Declaration duly filled out, demand a Receipt which later will be replaced by a CADASTRAL CERTIFICATE. This Certificate, to be sent out by IBRA, is indispensible to, among other things:
   - a) obtaining official credit and financing
   - b) receiving a guarantee of minimum prices in the marketing of your products
   - c) getting various forms of Technical Assistance
   - d) being able to divide, rent, sell, mortgage or otherwise dispose of your property
   - e) facilitating division of goods among heirs.

10) If you think you are entitled to a reduction of or exemption from the Rural Land Tax (Articles 30 to 32, Decree 56,792 published in the Diário Oficial da União on 8-31-1965) apply to IBRA mentioning the number of the Declaration Delivery Receipt pertaining to your property and submitting documents to prove your claim.

11) The property owner who is up to date in the payment of his Rural Property Tax will not only avoid larger payments he will also be able to make ample use of his CADASTRAL CERTIFICATE for the things specified above (Article 56, Decree 56,972 published in the Diário Oficial da União on 8-31-1965)

12) All information given should refer to the year 1965 except for the amount of ITR paid in 1964.

RURAL PROPERTY for this Declaration means a property of contiguous area formed by one or more parcels of land held by the same owner or owners regardless of size or locale, whether urban perimeter, suburban or rural, and which is or is capable of being developed for vegetable-extractive, agricultural, grazing or agro-industrial activities.

Sale price (two copies) CR$ (two hundred cruzeiros)

ANNEXES TO THIS DECLARATION					LOCALE OF PROPERTY	IDENTIFICATION OF PROPERTY	Do not fill in the lined spaces. They are for IBRA's use.
#1	#2	#3	#4	In Order	Inventory Unit Stamp		

01 IDENTIFICATION AND LOCALE OF PROPERTY	Write in the name by which your property is known, as well as the State, County, District, and all other locations such as a road or railroad and the distance of the property from such a known point.
① Name of the Property ② State or Territory	
③ County ④ District	
⑤ Other Locational Designations	

02 COMPLETE NAME OF THE OWNER (LEGAL OR PHYSICAL PERSON)	Write in the complete name of the person or legal entity owning the property
1 Complete Name of the Single or Group Owner	

03 ADDRESS FOR CORRESPONDENCE	Give property's address or address of a correspondent in a city with regular postal service. It is in your interest not to omit this information.
① Post Office Box or Street Number	
② Locality ③ City ④ State	

04 CHARACTERISTICS OF THE OWNING ENTITY (CORPORATE PERSON)

If the owner is a corporate person give information about its constitution and present capital and mark with an "x" the square indicating the type of entity it is

① Date of constitution / /   ② Present registered capital Cr$ ③ Documentation of constitution and locale of registration and entry. Give book and page numbers

01	02	03	04	05	06
Individual?	Limited Corporation?	Corporation?	Mixed Corporation?	Foundation?	Religious Institution?

07	08	09	10	11	12
Educational or Philanthropic Organization?	Cooperative?	County Entity?	State Entity?	Federal Entity?	Other?

05 CHARACTERISTICS OF THE OWNER AS PHYSICAL PERSON (ALONE OR IN CONDOMINIUM)

Cite the documents that identify the person making the declaration

① Type of documentation for identification   Place issued   Registry number

Give the date of birth or naturalization of the person making the declaration

② Date of birth / /   Native Brazilian 1   Naturalized Brazilian 2   Foreigner 3   State (1) or country (2 and 3) in which born

Indicate by an "x" the highest educational level attained by the person making the declaration

③ Illiterate 0   Read and write only 1   Finished primary school 2   Finished grade school 3   Finished high school 4   College 5

Mark either the YES or NO square; if you have no family or dependents draw a line through the squares

Do you reside permanently on property? 1 0 YES NO	Do you take personal charge of work on the property? 1 0 YES NO	Do you have outside remunerative activities? 1 0 YES NO	If you have family and dependents on the property how many can work?	How many of these actually do work?

06 OWNERSHIP CONDITIONS

Mark an "X" in either the YES or NO square

① Do you possess all or part of another rural property in any other part of the country? 1 0 YES NO	② Do you maintain a resident administrator to direct work on this property? 1 0 YES NO	③ Does this property belong to more than one owner? 1 0 YES NO

Fill in only if there is more than one owner (condominium)

④ Are the owners heirs holding the property in common? 1 0 YES NO	⑤ How many owners are there including the person making the declaration?	⑥ Give the percentage of the property that is owned by the person making the declaration?

07 TENURE CONDITIONS ON THE PROPERTY

If your response to either item 2 or item 3 is YES then fill out the SHARECROPPER and/or RENTER annexes

① Do you maintain salaried workers on the property? 1 0 YES NO	② Do you have sharecropping arrangements on any part of the property? 1 0 YES NO	③ Do you rent out all or any part of the property? 1 0 YES NO

08 CONDITIONS OF WAGE LABORERS ON THE PROPERTY

Pay special attention to these questions. If you have no wage laborers and do not expect to have draw a line through the places calling for an answer

① How many wage laborers are permanently employed on the property?	② What is the largest number of wage laborers employed in periods of heaviest labor need?	③ Do you maintain a register of wage laborers?

④ Do you maintain a stock of foods to supply the wage laborers? 1 0 YES NO	⑤ Do you provide land for wage laborers to grow their own food? 1 0 YES NO	⑥ Do you forbid pay-ment of wage laborers in the form of scrip, etc.? 1 0 YES NO	⑦ Do you maintain receipts of pay-ments to wage laborers? 1 0 YES NO

09 HABITATION AND SANITATION CONDITIONS

Give careful attention to the information requested here even though it relates only to the dwelling of the person making the declaration

① How many families reside on the property?	② How many dwellings are on the property?	③ How many persons reside in all these houses?	④ What is the total number of bedrooms among the houses on the property?

⑤ How many of the houses have clay or mud walls?	⑥ How many of the houses have bare dirt floors?	⑦ How many houses have a well, spring or faucet within 100 meters?	⑧ How many latrines or septic tanks are on the property?

10 EDUCATIONAL CONDITIONS

How many minors (between the ages of 7 and 14) live on the property and of these how many are in school and what type of facilities does the person making the declaration provide for them?

① How many minors between 7 and 14 reside on the property?	② How many minors between 7 and 14 attend school?	③ Does the owner maintain a school? 1 0 YES NO	④ Does the owner supply school materials? 1 0 YES NO

⑤ Does the owner help to support a teacher? 1 0 YES NO	⑥ Does the owner furnish transpor-tation for the pupils? 1 0 YES NO	⑦ Does the owner supply school lunches? 1 0 YES NO	⑧ Does the owner supply clothes or shoes to the pupils? 1 0 YES NO

11 TECHNICAL LEVEL

Mark the appropriate square with an "x"

① Do you keep books of expenditures and receipts on the property? 1 0 YES NO	② Do you promote conservation by terracing or contour plow-ing or by applying other erosion control techniques? 1 0 YES NO	③ Do you select seeds cross-breed plants and use artificial insemination? 1 0 YES NO

④ Do you rotate crops or pastures or replant forests? 1 0 YES NO	⑤ Do you innoculate animals and use insecticides on plants? 1 0 YES NO	⑥ Do you use mechanical equip-ment to cut trees, to plant and harvest crops, to treat animals and to fight forest fires? 1 0 YES NO

12 CONDITIONS OF ACCESS TO THE PROPERTY

Give the city or locale where you usually sell your products and the distance in kilometers from your property to that place

Name of the city or locale where you usually sell your products and the distance in kilometers from your property to that place   Total distance in kilometers you have to travel

① Roads passable only to beasts of burden	② Waterways passable only to hand-powered craft	③ Roads at best pass-able to horse and ox-carts.	④ Waterways or lakes passable to motorboats

Give the distances you must travel on the various types of routes

⑤ Roads at best passable to vehicles with four-wheel drive (jeep or pick-up)	⑥ Rivers or lakes with regu-larly scheduled boats	7 Railroads; Roads, paved or not, but passable to any kind of vehicle.	Note: Do Not Fill Out

Indicate the conditions that impede the flow of your goods to market

How many days per year is access to the above-mentioned market interrupted?   In what month is access worst or impracticable?   Does this interruption coincide with the harvest? 1 0 YES NO

13 DESTINATION OF THE PRINCIPAL PRODUCT OF THE PROPERTY

The "principal product" is that which characterizes the operation of your farm

Processed on property 1	Sold to middleman 2	Sold to wholesaler 3	Sold to retailer 4	Sold to cooperative 5	Sold to govern-ment agency 6	Sold to consumers 7

NOTE:

1. Because of the wide variance in measure of area from region to region in the country, the HECTARE (Ha) which corresponds to 10,000 square meters is established as the SOLE unit of area measure for this declaration. The "Alqueire geometrico" or "Alqueire mineiro", for example, contains 48,400 square meters or 4.84 Ha; the "quadra do campo" or "quadra do sesmaria" contains 871,200 square meters or 87.12 Ha; the "Tarefa", "mil covas" or "linha" contains 625 square braças or 3,025 square meters or 0.3 Ha.
   If you encounter difficulty in converting to Hectares get help from the "local agent of the County Survey Unit."

2. For the reasons given above the metric ton and its fractions in kilograms is adopted as the only unit of weight to measure quantity of production (bloc 19). Note that banana production is measured in stems, orange production in hundreds.

Indicate the areas in hectares rounded to the nearest tenth.

Draw a line through those spaces which do not apply to production on your property.

14 AREAS UTILIZED FOR PRODUCTION (Hectares)

Total area utilized for FRUIT AND TRUCK CROPS	①	,	.
Total area utilized for PERMANENT CROPS	②	,	.
Total area utilized for TEMPORARY CROPS	③	,	.
Total area utilized for GRAZING SMALL ANIMALS	④	,	.
Total area utilized for GRAZING LARGE ANIMALS	⑤	,	.
Total area utilized for FORESTRY	⑥	,	.

The TOTAL AREA OF THE PROPERTY (item 4) is equal to the sum of items 1, 2 and 3 as well as items 5 and 6. UNUSEABLE AREA is understood to mean area which is not capable of being used for any one of the crops specified in bloc 14. Item 6 is the sum of items 7 and 8.

15 DISTRIBUTION OF AREAS ON THE PROPERTY (Ha.)

Total area controlled by owner	①	,	.
Total area sharecropped	②	,	.
Total area rented	③	,	.
Total area of property	④	,	.
Total unuseable area	⑤	,	.
Total useable area	⑥	,	.
Total area utilized	⑦	,	.
Total useable area that is not used	⑧	,	.

The percentages requested refer to the relationship between the parcel of the type specified and the USEABLE AREA (item 6 of bloc 5).

16 CLASSIFICATION OF IMPROVED LANDS

topography type	Level %	Undulating %	Rough %	Totals
Forest or First Class Land				
Scrub Forest or Second Class Land				
Grassland or Third Class Land				
Totals				100%

Give the present value of the unimproved land (excluding the improvements specified in items 2 through 7); then total the value of improvements. Two tenths of one percent (0.2%) of the VALUE OF THE UNIMPROVED LAND makes up the alíquota basica, a major ingredient of the RURAL LAND TAX.

17 VALUE OF PROPERTY AND IMPROVEMENTS (Cr$)

Value of Unimproved Land	①	
Value of buildings	②	
Value of mechanical equipment	③	
Value of special installations	④	
Value of permanent crops	⑤	
Value of animals	⑥	
Value of natural or planted trees	⑦	
Total value of improvements	⑧	
Value of Property and Improvements	⑨	

(left side label: Value of improvements)

Calculate the value of the property's total output in 1965 (item 4) taking as a base the prices common to the region and distribute these values among items 1, 2 and 3. By LOST OUTPUT is meant production whether harvested or not which is not stored or sold.

Distribute item 4 among items 5 and 6 if you have SHARECROPPERS or RENTERS.

18 VALUE OF OUTPUT (Cr$)

Value of output SOLD	①	
Value of output CONSUMED or STORED	②	
Value of output LOST	③	
Value of Total Output	④	
Value of output from areas under control of the owner	⑤	
Value of output from areas sharecropped	⑥	
Value of output from areas rented out	⑦	

---

19 INFORMATION ON BASIC CROPS

Product		Area Cultivated (Ha)	Quantity Produced	
TREE COTTON tons	⑪		ton	kg
BANANAS tons	⑫		ton	kg
CACAO tons	⑬		ton	kg
COFFEE tons	⑭		ton	kg
ORANGES hundreds	⑮		ton	kg
GRAPES tons	⑯		ton	kg
COTTON tons	⑳		ton	kg
PEANUTS tons	㉑		ton	kg
RICE tons	㉒		ton	kg
POTATOES tons	㉓		ton	kg
SUGAR CANE tons	㉔		ton	kg
BEANS tons	㉕		ton	kg
TOBACCO tons	㉖		ton	kg
MANDIOCA tons	㉗		ton	kg
CORN tons	㉘		ton	kg
WHEAT tons	㉙		ton	kg

		Area Pastured	No. of Head
Large Animals COWS	㉚		

		Wool Produced (kg)	No. of Head
Medium Animals SHEEP	㉛		

For the crops listed to the left give the area cultivated and the quantity produced in 1965. Your answers should refer to crops before their processing and to the area cultivated in hectares. Fractions of hectares should be placed to the right of the point.

Give the property's total production, that under control of the OWNER as well as that under control of SHARECROPPERS and RENTERS. Fractions of hectares should be placed to the right of the point.

In item 30 give the area of natural and planted pasture and the number of cows; in item 31, the quantity in kilograms of wool produced and the number of sheep.

---

20 RURAL CREDIT CONDITIONS

You do not borrow?	00 ☐	You borrow for crops?	1 ☐	You borrow for animals?	2 ☐

IF YOU BORROW INDICATE THE SOURCE OF FINANCE

Bank of Brazil?	1 ☐	state bank	2 ☐	government institute	3 ☐
private bank?	4 ☐	development institute?	5 ☐	cooperative?	6 ☐
private source?	7 ☐				

Mark an "x" if you do not borrow, or if you do, mark the type of credit. Do the same for the source of the credit

---

21 SALES TAX

Did you pay this tax in 1965?	YES 1 ☐	NO 0 ☐	If so, how much was it? Cr$

Indicate by an "x" whether you paid the Sales Tax in 1965 and the amount you paid.

---

22 RURAL PROPERTY TAX

Did you pay this tax in 1964?	YES 1 ☐	NO 0 ☐	Did you pay this tax in 1965?	YES 1 ☐	NO 0 ☐

---

23 DETAILS OF PAYMENT OF RURAL PROPERTY TAX

County Where Paid		% of Area	Amount Paid (Cr$)
1964 Tax		%	
		%	
		%	
	Total Tax Paid in 1964		
1965 Tax		%	
		%	
		%	
	Total Tax Paid in 1965		

Indicate by an "x" if you paid the Rural Land Tax in 1964 and 1965, and indicate in bloc 23 the amounts paid in each year. If you paid in more than one county indicate the percentage of the area of the property in each county and the amount paid in each.

149

24   MEANS BY WHICH YOU OBTAINED THE PROPERTY

Mark an "x" in the square that corresponds to the means by which you obtained the property (1 through 11) or if you simply occupy the property (item 12).

Supply the explanations you deem necessary.

Promise to purchase?	01 ☐	Private sale?	02 ☐	Purchase of lot in private colony?	03 ☐	Purchase of lot in government colony?	04 ☐	Gift or sale of public lands?	05 ☐	By exchange of property?	06 ☐
By indemnification or compensation?	07 ☐	By social or marriage contract?	08 ☐	Foreclosure?	09 ☐	Inherited?	10 ☐	Land grant based on occupance?	11 ☐	Simply the occupant?	12 ☐

Additional Comments on the Means by Which You Obtained the Property

25   DOCUMENT OR TITLE OF OWNERSHIP

Mark an "x" in the square that indicates the type of DOCUMENT which you hold.

Private document?	1 ☐	Public contract?	2 ☐	Will?	3 ☐	Social contract?	4 ☐	Government act?	5 ☐

Additional comments on the document or title of ownership

Locale of registration and entry. Give book and page numbers.

26   AREAS AND BOUNDARIES GIVEN IN THE TITLE

Give the area of the property in the units of measure shown in the title or document and convert this to hectares.

Area given in the document in units of measure used therein.		Actual area converted to hectares	

Give the boundaries, names of neighboring properties and extent of frontage on public routes

Copy from the document or title the boundaries, names of neighboring properties, extent of frontage on public routes and all other related information.

If the rural property is made up of various areas each with separate titles or documents fill out annex No. 4 for each of the additional titles.

It is imperative that this declaration be signed by the owner or his duly authorized proxy.
The proxy should supply information about the owner who for all intents and purposes is considered the person making this declaration.

I declare to be true all the information given by me or under my authority in this DECLARATION OF PROPERTY in full recognition of the requirements and penalties laid out in Paragraph 3 of Article 49 of Law No. 4504 (Estatuto da Terra) dated November 30, 1964, in Article 7 of Law No. 4357 (Monetary Correction) dated July 16, 1961 and in Article 4 of Law No. 4729 dated July 14, 1965.

Locale_____ Date_____

_____
Signature of the owner or his proxy
(If the owner is represented by a proxy attach a power-of-attorney annex)

APPENDIX B

Sample Modulo Calculations

The Grupo de Regulamentação do Estatuto da Terra (GRET) worked out the size in hectares of each of the fifty-four modulos (one for each of the six land uses in each of the nine physiographic zones). The following formula was used:

$$\text{modulo size in hectares} = \frac{67.2\,A}{B-(C+.225D)}$$

where,

A = Minimum Salary

> The 67.2 multiplier is the product of 4 adults x 12 months x 1.4 (the 40% increment necessary for a person to participate fully in society).

B = Income per Hectare per Year (Yield per hectare per year x Minimum price)

C = Out-of-Pocket Costs per Hectare per Year

D = Land Value

> The .225 multiplier is the product of the unimproved value of the land x 1.5 (land + improvements = 1.5 x the value of the unimproved land) x .15 return on the total capital investment.

GRET used whatever data were available to determine the modulo sizes. The following pages present some of the modulo calculations.

CALCULATION OF THE MODULO FOR MARKET GARDENING
(Market Gardening)

Intensive agriculture
State, Guanabara
Year, 1962
US$ = Cr$ 400

1. Minimum Salary = Cr$ 645,120

    Cr$ 9,600 x 67.2

2. Income = Cr$ 354,964

    Total value of production = Cr$ 80,541,300 divided by the 226.9
    hectares in the farm used as the example

3. Out-of-Pocket Costs = Cr$ 54,754

	Cr$/hectare/year
seeds and seedlings	18,202
animal fertilizers	21,577
chemical fertilizers	7,748
insecticides	5,850
fuels and lubricants	1,377
	54,754

4. Land Value = Cr$ 22,500

    Cr$ 100,000 x .225

5. Modulo

$$\frac{654,120}{354,964 - (54,754 + 22,500} = \frac{654,120}{277,710}$$

2.3 hectares

CALCULATION OF THE MODULO FOR CULTIVATION OF ORANGES
(Perennial Crop)

Intensive agriculture
State, Rio de Janeiro
   Municipio, Itaboraí
Year, 1964/65
US$ = Cr$ 1,800

1. Minimum Salary = Cr$ 4,435,200

    Cr$ 66,000 x 67.2

2. Income = Cr$ 657,000

    Yield: 1,095 boxes per hectare
    Minimum price: Cr$ 600 per box

3. Out-of-Pocket Costs = Cr$ 50,600

	Cr$/hectare/year
seedlings	4,800
fertilization	43,800
cultivation	2,000
	50,600

4. Land Value = Cr$ 45,000

    Cr$ 200,000 per hectare x .225

5. Modulo

$$\frac{4,435,200}{657,000 - (50,600 + 45,000)} \quad = \quad \frac{4,435,200}{561,400}$$

7.9 hectares

CALCULATION OF THE MODULO FOR COFFEE CULTIVATION
(Perennial Crop)

Heavily fertilized
State, São Paulo
Year, 1964–65
US$ = Cr$ 1,800

1. Minimum Salary = Cr$ 4,435,200

    Cr$ 66,000 × 67.2

2. Income = Cr$ 900,000

    Yield: 3,000 kilograms per hectare
    Minimum price: Cr$ 300 per kilogram

3. Out-of-Pocket Costs = Cr$ 242,263

	Cr$/hectares/year
Materials	
chemical fertilizers	228,560
seedlings for re-planting	2,000
sacks, tools and utensils	1,520
	232,080
Transportation	
carts, per day per hectare	2,160
animals, per day per hectare	10,183
	12,343
Total	Cr$ 244,423

4. Land Value = Cr$ 69,750

    Cr$ 310,000 per hectare × .225

5. Modulo

$$\frac{4,435,200}{900,000 - (244,423 + 69,750)} = \frac{4,435,200}{585,827}$$

7.5 hectares

156

CALCULATION OF THE MODULO FOR COFFEE CULTIVATION
(Perennial Crop)

Without fertilizer
State, São Paulo
Year, 1964/65
US$ = Cr$ 1,800

1. Minimum Salary = Cr$ 4,435,200

   Cr$ 66,000 x 67.2

2. Income Cr$ 228,000

   Yield: 760 kilograms per hectare
   Minimum price: Cr$ 300 per kilogram

3. Out-of-Pocket Costs = Cr$ 14,164

   Materials
   seedlings for re-planting   5,000
   sacks   1,520
                                      6,520

   Transportation
   carts, days per hectare   1,620
   animals, days per hectare   6,024
                                      7,644

            Total   14,164

4. Land Value = Cr$ 69,750

   Cr$ 310,000 per hectare x .225

5. Modulo

$$\frac{4,435,200}{228,000 - (14,164 + 69,750)} = \frac{4,435,200}{144,086}$$

31.0 hectares

CALCULATION OF THE MODULO FOR BLACK PEPPER CULTIVATION
(Perennial Crop)

Hand labor
State, Pará
Year, 1960
US$ = Cr$ 185

1. Minimum Salary = Cr$ 403,000

    Cr$ 6,000 x 67.2

2. Income = Cr$ 560,000

    Yield: 1,750 kilograms per hectare
    Minimum price: Cr$ 320 per kilogram

3. Out-of-Pocket Costs = Cr$ 25,000

    fertilizers, fungicides, insecticides
    contingencies

    Cr$/hectare/year

    15,000
    10,000
    ‾‾‾‾‾‾
    25,000

4. Land Value = Cr$ 5,625

    Cr$ 25,000 per hectare x .225

5. Modulo

$$\frac{403,200}{560,000 - (25,000 + 5,625)} = \frac{403,200}{529,375}$$

0.8 hectares

CALCULATION OF THE MODULO FOR BEAN CULTIVATION
(Temporary Crop)

Animal power
State, São Paulo
Year, 1963/64
US$ = Cr$ 1,500

1. Minimum Salary = Cr$ 1,411,200

    Cr$ 21,000 x 67.2

2. Income = Cr$ 105,400

    Yield: 17 sacks of 60 kilograms per hectare
    Minimum price: Cr$ 6,200 per sack

3. Out-of-Pocket Costs = Cr$ 29,800

	Cr$/hectare/year
operations	5,500
seed	9,300
fertilizer	15,000
	29,800

4. Land Value = Cr$ 22,500

    Cr$ = 100,000 per hectare x .225

5. Modulo

$$\frac{1,411,200}{105,400 - (29,800 + 22,500)} = \frac{1,411,200}{53,100}$$

26.5 hectares

CALCULATION OF THE MODULO FOR IRRIGATED RICE CULTIVATION
(Temporary Crop)

Animal power
State, São Paulo
Year, 1962/63
US$ = Cr$ 600

1. Minimum Salary + Cr$ 645,120

   Cr$ 9,600 x 67.2

2. Income = Cr$ 217,580

   Yield: 43 sacks of 60 kilograms each per hectare
   Minimum price: Cr$ 5,060 per sack

3. Out-of-Pocket Costs = Cr$ 33,970

	Cr$/hectare/year
plowing	9,374
seeds	7,273
fertilizer	12,985
sacks and cord	4,338
	33,970

4. Land Value = Cr$ 27,000

   Cr$ 120,000 per hectare x .225

5. Modulo

$$\frac{645,120}{217,580 - (33,970 + 27,000)} = \frac{645,120}{156,610}$$

4.0 hectares

CALCULATION OF THE MODULO FOR NON-IRRIGATED RICE CULTIVATION
(Temporary Crop)

Animal power
State, São Paulo
Year, 1963/64
US$ = Cr$ 1,500

1. Minimum Salary = Cr$ 1,411,200

    Cr$ 21,000 x 67.2

2. Income = 150,908

    Yield: 31 sacks of 60 kilograms each per hectare
    Minimum price: Cr$ 4,868

3. Out-of-Pocket Costs = Cr$ 18,657

	Cr$/hectare/year
seeds	4,297
fertilizer	14,360
	18,657

4. Land Value = Cr$ 33,750

    Cr$ 150,000 per hectare x .225

5. Modulo

$$\frac{1,411,200}{150,908 - (18,657 + 33,750)} = \frac{1,411,200}{98,501}$$

14.0 hectares

CALCULATION OF THE MODULO FOR CULTIVATION OF WHEAT
(Temporary Crop)

Mechanized
State, Rio Grande do Sul
Year, 1962/63
US$ = Cr$ 600

1. Minimum Salary = Cr$ 645,120

    Cr$ 9,600 × 67.2

2. Income = Cr$ 105,000

    Yield: 1.5 tons per hectare
    Minimum price: Cr$ 70,000 per ton

3. Out-of-Pocket Costs = Cr$ 31,708

	Cr$/ hectare/year
preparing the land	5,589
planting and fertilizing	4,668
seeds	3,306
fertilizers	17,525
insecticides	620
	31,708

4. Land Value = Cr$ 18,000

    Cr$ 81,000 per hectare × .225

5. Modulo

$$\frac{645,120}{105,000 - (31,708 + 18,000)} = \frac{645,120}{55,292}$$

12.0 hectares

CALCULATION OF THE MODULO FOR CULTIVATION OF CORN
(Temporary Crop)

Animal power
State, São Paulo
Year, 1963/64
US$ = Cr$ 1,500

1. Minimum Salary = Cr$ 1,411,200

    Cr$ 21,000 x 67.2

2. Income = Cr$ 120,700

    Yield: 50 sacks of 60 kilograms each per hectare
    Minimum price: Cr$ 2,414 per sack

3. Out-of-Pocket Costs = Cr$ 32,182

	Cr$/hectare/year
plowing and fertilizer	6,083
seed	967
chemical fertilizer	25,132
	32,182

4. Land Value = Cr$ 22,500

    Cr$ 100,000 per hectare x .225

5. Modulo

$$\frac{1,411,200}{120,700 - (32,182 + 22,500)} = \frac{1,411,200}{66,018}$$

21.0 hectares

CALCULATION OF THE MODULO FOR SUGAR CANE CULTIVATION
(Temporary Crop)

Mechanized
State, São Paulo
Year, 1965
US$ = Cr$ 1,800

1. Minimum Salary = Cr$ 4,435,200

    Cr$ 66,000 × 67.2

2. Income = Cr$ 759,360

    Yield: 70 tons per hectare
    Minimum price: Cr$ 10,848 per ton

3. Out-of-Pocket Costs = Cr$ 59,210

	Cr$/hectare/year
fertilizer	24,150
materials	310
machinery	33,040
other	1,710
	59,210

4. Land Value = Cr$ 78,750

    Cr$ 350,000 per hectare × .225

5. Modulo

$$\frac{4,435,200}{759,360 - (59,210 + 78,750)} = \frac{4,435,200}{621,400}$$

7.0 hectares

CALCULATION OF THE MODULO FOR SUGAR CANE CULTIVATION
(Temporary Crop)

Animal power
State, Pernambuco
Year, 1963
US$ = Cr$ 1,000

1. Minimum Salary = Cr$ 1,411,200

    Cr$ 21,000 × 67.2

2. Income = Cr$ 299,600

    Yield: 42.8 tons per hectare
    Minimum price: Cr$ 7,000 per ton

3. Out–of–Pocket Costs = Cr$ 19,108

	Cr$/hectare/year
machinery	188
animals	3,222
fertilizer	8,153
chemicals	7,488
seeds	57
	19,108

4. Land Value = Cr$ 14,625

    Cr$ 65,000 per hectare × .225

5. Modulo

$$\frac{1,411,200}{299,600 - (19,108 + 14,625)} = \frac{1,411,200}{265,867}$$

5.3 hectares

CALCULATION OF THE MODULO FOR TOBACCO CULTIVATION
(Temporary Crop)

Mechanized
State, Rio Grande do Sul
Year, 1960–61
US$ = Cr$ 225

1. Minimum Salary = Cr$ 403,200

   Cr$ 6,000 x 67.2

2. Income = Cr$ 84,000

   Yield: 800 kilograms per hectare
   Minimum price: Cr$ 105 per kilogram

3. Out-of-Pocket Costs = Cr$ 14,820

	Cr$/hectare/year
land preparation	1,100
fertilization	8,600
preparation of seedlings	4,770
seeds	350
	14,820

4. Land Value = Cr$ 4,500

   Cr$ 20,000 per hectare x .225

%. Modulo

$$\frac{403,200}{84,000 - (14,820 + 4,500)} = \frac{403,200}{64,680}$$

6.2 hectares

CALCULATION OF THE MODULO FOR COTTON CULTIVATION
(Temporary Crop)

Mechanized
State, São Paulo
Year, 1963/64
US$ = Cr$ 1,500

1. Minimum Salary = Cr$ = 1,411,200

   Cr$ 21,000 x 67.2

2. Income = Cr$ 154,440

   Yield: 66 arrobas of 15 kilograms each per hectare
   Minimum price: Cr$ 2,340 per arroba

3. Out-of-Pocket Costs = Cr$ 51,801

	Cr$/hectare/year
plowing	7,304
terracing	1,827
transportation	1,827
fertilizer	20,702
seeds	5,100
insecticides	15,041
	51,801

4. Land Value = Cr$ 33,750

   Cr$ 150,000 per hectare x .225

5. Modulo

$$\frac{1,411,600}{154,440 - (51,801 + 33,750)} = \frac{1,411,600}{68,889}$$

20.0 hectares

CALCULATION OF THE MODULO FOR PRODUCTION OF SWINE
(Small Livestock)

State, Rio de Janeiro
Year, 1965
US$ = Cr$ 1,800

1. Minimum Salary = Cr$ 4,435,200

   Cr$ 66,000 x 67.2

2. Income = Cr$ 488,800

   Yield: 561 kilograms per hectare
   Minimum price: Cr$ 800 per kilogram

3. Out-of-Pocket Costs = Cr$ 66314

   Assuming 1.5 kilograms of ration per each 50 kilograms of live
   weight pig and assuming corn to make up 36.5% of the ration,
   soybean meal 58.5% and mandioca 5% we have:

	Cr$/hectare/year
corn	11,746
soybean meal	31,337
mandioca	5,537
tankage	14,830
vaccines	2,864
	66,314

4. Land Value = Cr$ 22,500

   Cr$ 100,000 per hectare x .225

5. Modulo

$$\frac{4,435,200}{448,800 - (66,314 + 22,500)} = \frac{4,435,200}{359,986}$$

12.0 hectares

CALCULATION OF THE MODULO FOR GRAZING CATTLE
(Large Livestock)

Natural pasture
Region, East
Year, 1965
US$ = Cr$ 1,800
Carrying capacity 0.5 head per hectare

1. Minimum Salary = Cr$ 4,435,200

   Cr$ 66,000 x 67.2

2. Income = Cr$ 103,500

   Yield: averaging a gain in weight of one kilogram per day per head, the annual gain is 180 kilograms
   Minimum price: Cr$ 575 per kilogram

3. Out–of–Pocket Costs

	Cr$/hectare/year
salt	1,200
vaccine	250
other	850
	2,300

4. Land Value = Cr$ 45,000

   Cr$ 200,000 per hectare x .225

5. Modulo

$$\frac{4,435,200}{103,500 - (2,300 + 45,000)} = \frac{4,435,200}{56,200}$$

79.0 hectares

CALCULATION OF THE MODULO FOR PRODUCTION OF MILK
(Large Livestock)

> Natural pasture
> Location, Paraíba Valley
> Year, 1965
> Herd, 90 head – 60 producing, 30 dry
> Daily production, 5 liters per head
> Total daily production, 300 liters

1. Minimum Salary = Cr$ 4,435,200

    Cr$ 66,000 x 67.2

2. Income = Cr$ 281,175

    Yield: at two head per hectare, daily production would be 10 liters per hectare, but only 2/3 of the herd is producing so the yield is cut to 6.7 liters per hectare per day and this works out to 2,445 liters per hectare per year.

    Minimum price: Cr$ 115 per liter

3. Out-of-Pocket Costs = Cr$ 92,968

	Cr$/hectare/year
salt	7,992
vaccine	1,000
balanced ration	63,996
minerals and bone meal	3,996
medicines	10,656
electrical energy and fuel	5,328
	92,968

4. Land Value = Cr$ 45,000

    Cr$ 200,000 per hectare x .225

5. Modulo

$$\frac{4,435,200}{281,175 - (92,968 + 45,000)} = \frac{4,435,200}{143,207}$$

31.0 hectares

CALCULATION OF THE MODULO FOR EUCALYPTUS CULTIVATION
(Forestry)

State, Sao Paulo
Year, 1965
US$ = Cr$ 1,800

1. Minimum Salary = Cr$ 4,435,200

    Cr$ 66,000 x 67.2

2. Income = Cr$ 400,000

    Yield: 200 cubic meters per hectare
    Minimum price: Cr$ 2,000 per cubic meter

3. Out-of-Pocket Costs = Cr$ 17,036

	Cr$/hectare/year
insecticides	5,850
internal transportation	10,000
seeds	1,186
	17,036

4. Land Value = Cr$ 11,250

    Cr$ 50,000 per hectare x .225

5. Modulo

$$\frac{4,435,200}{400,000 - (17,036 + 11,250)} = \frac{4,435,200}{371,714} = 12 \text{ hectares}$$

Since it takes seven years to bring eucalyptus into production the final modulo must equal seven times the one above or

84 hectares

APPENDIX C

The Coefficient of Location

The Coefficient of Location (CL) reflects not only a holding's difficulty and reliability of access to market, but also the aggregate transportation conditions in the physiographic zone in which the property is located. The former two conditions are expressed as the Difficulty of Access Factor (DAF) and the Reliability of Access Factor (RAF), and the latter as the Location Index.

The Difficulty of Access Factor

Each propertyowner indicates on his questionnaire the distance in kilometers his produce must travel over certain types of access routes to get to market (Table 1). Depending upon its length, each route-type is assigned a difficulty-of-access degree, ranging from 0 to .5 (there is no .4). The degrees are then added to yield the Difficulty of Access Score (DAS), which cannot exceed .5. The DAS is then subtracted from 2.5, a constant, to give the DAF, whose range is 2.0 to 2.5 in units of .1.

As an example of this operation, let us say that a property reaches its market over 4 kilometers of oxcart roads (degree of access = .2) and 19 kilometers of badly rutted roads which require use of a 4-wheel-drive truck (degree of access = .1). The property's DAS = .3 (.2 + .1); its DAF = 2.2 (2.5 - .3). But a property whose produce moves, say, 7 kilometers on beasts of burden (.3) and then 10 kilometers by barge (.3) would not receive a DAS of .6, because the maximum allowable is .5. The DAF in this case would be 2.0 (2.5 - .5).

The Reliability of Access Factor

A property's reliability of access to market depends upon when and for how long this access is interrupted. Each of five interruption periods is assigned a value that depends upon its length and whether it occurs during the harvest season (Table 2). The harvest and nonharvest values are added to yield the Reliability of Access Score (RAS) which may not exceed 1.0. The RAS is subtracted from a constant, 4.0, to produce the RAF.

For example, a property's access to market may be interrupted for 10 days just before harvest (interruption value = .2) and ten days during harvest (interruption value = .4), resulting in an RAS of .6 (.2 + .4) and an RAF of 3.4 (4.0 - .6).

TABLE 1

Determining the Difficulty of Access Factor

Nature of the Access Route	Degree of Difficulty of Access				
	.5	.3	.2	.1	0
Roads passable only to beasts of burden Waterways passable only to hand-powered craft	more than 10 kms.	0 to 10	0	0	0
Roads at best passable to horse and ox-carts Waterways or lakes passable to motor boats	more than 20 kms.	5 to 20	less than 5 kms.	0	0
Roads at best passable to vehicles with 4 wheel drive (jeep or pick-up) Rivers or lakes with regularly scheduled boats	more than 100 kms.	50 to 100	20 to 49	less than 20 kms.	0
Railroads Roads, paved or not, passable to any kind of vehicle	more than 200 kms.	100 to 200	70 to 99	40 to 69	less than 40 kms.

176

TABLE 2

Reliability of Access

Length of Interruption in Days	Occurrence of Interruption	
	Harvest	Non-harvest
None	0	0
0 - 15	0.2	0.4
16 - 30	0.4	0.8
31 - 60	0.8	1.0
more than 60	1.0	1.0

TABLE 3

Translating the Location Factor into
the Coefficient of Location

Location Factor	Coefficient of Location
Less than 50	1.0
50 - 99	1.1
100 - 149	1.2
150 - 199	1.3
200 - 249	1.4
250 - 299	1.5
More than 300	1.6

The sum of harvest and nonharvest interruption
values may actually reach 2.0, but the upper allowable limit of the RAS is 1.0. Thus, the RAF ranges
from 3.0 (4.0 - 1.0) to 4.0 (4.0 - 0) in units of
.1.

Location Index

Each physiographic zone is assigned a Location
Index, which varies with a zone's topography, population potential, and proximity to urban markets,
and is closely linked to the average value per
hectare of unimproved land in a zone. The Index
ranges from 300 in the zones around the cities of
Rio de Janeiro and São Paulo to 70 in a zone in Acre
state in the upper Amazon basin. For Bragança
Paulista, the Location Index is 220.

Determining the CL

To find the Coefficient of Location, the DAF is
multiplied by the RAF and the result divided by 10.
This may yield a maximum product (meaning very good
access routes and reliability)of 1.0 (DAF of 2.5 x
RAF of 4.0 = 10/10 = 1.0) or a minimum product
(meaning very poor access and reliability) of .6
(DAF of 2.0 x RAF of 3.0 = 6.0/10 = .6).

This figure is now multiplied by the Location
Index of the zone to yield the Location Factor,
which is then translated into the Coefficient of
Location (Table 3), which ranges from 1.0 to 1.6 in
units of .1. Examples of this calculation follow:

1. A property in Bragança Paulista (LI of 220)
with maximum ease and reliability of access (DAF
of 2.5 x RAF of 4.0 = 10/10 = 1.0) will have a
Location Factor of 220 (1.0 x 220), which translates
to a CL of 1.4.
2. A Bragança Paulista property with maximum
difficulty and poorest possible reliability of access
(DAF of 2.0 x RAF of 3.0 = 6.0/10 = .6)will have a
Location Factor of 132 (.6 x 220),which translates to
a CL of 1.2.

Logic, Structure, and Application of the CL

Even though the value of the CL is completely
beyond control of the propertyowner, it has a
greater potential for raising the Rural Land Tax
than any of the other three coefficients. Any of

the other coefficient-multipliers may be below 1.0,
thereby fractioning the tax. But the CL is always
at or above 1.0, thus either acting neutrally (at
1.0) or raising the tax by as much as 60 per cent
(at 1.6), but never reducing it. For any property
in a given zone, the CL is at the mercy of the
aggregate of access conditions in that zone. If
these conditions are good, a propertyowner is faced
with a high Location Index and a potentially high CL.
If his property's ease and reliability of access are
also good, his CL will be high. Such a location and
access conditions would certainly seem to warrant
an investment in the holding great enough to reduce
the value of the other three coefficients. The
necessity to compensate for a high CL is felt most
acutely by owners of unused circumurban properties,
many of which are held for speculative purposes.

SELECTED BIBLIOGRAPHY

SELECTED BIBLIOGRAPHY

American International Association for Economic and
    Social Development (AIA) and U. S. Agency for
    International Development (AID). Survey of
    the Agricultural Potential of the Central
    Plateau of Brazil. Rio de Janeiro: 1963.

Andrade, Manoel Correia de. A terra e o homem no
    nordeste. São Paulo: Editora Brasiliense,
    1963.

Blalock, Hubert M. Social Statistics. New York:
    McGraw-Hill, 1960.

Caldeira, Clovis. Arrendamento e parceria no Brasil.
    Rio de Janeiro: Comissão Nacional de Política
    Agrária, 1955.

Carroll, Thomas F. "The Land Reform Issue in Latin
    America." Latin American Issues. Edited by
    A. O. Hirschman. New York: Twentieth Century
    Fund, 1961.

Comite Interamericano de Desenvolvimento Agricola.
    Posse e uso da terra e desenvolvimento sócio-
    econômico de setor agrícola - Brasil.
    Washington: Uniao Pan-Americana, Secretaria
    Geral de Organização dos Estados Americanos,
    1966.

Council on Foreign Relations. Social Change in
    Latin America Today. New York: Harper, 1960.

Delgado, Oscar, ed. Reformas agrárias en la America
    Latina. Mexico City: Fondo de Cultura
    Economica, 1965.

de Sousa, João Gonçalves. "Aspects of Land Tenure
    Problems in Latin America," Rural Sociology
    XXV, 1 (1960), 26-37.

Diegues, Manuel, Jr. Populacão e propriedade da
    terra no Brasil. Washington: União Pan-
    Americana, 1959.

Ettori, O. J. Thomazini. "Mão-de-obra na agri-
    cultura em São Paulo: Categorias, Remuneracão
    Legislação," Agricultura em São Paulo. VII, 12
    (December, 1961).

Food and Agricultural Organization of the United
    Nations. Interrelationship Between Agrarian
    Reform and Agricultural Development. Rome:
    1953.

Frank, Andrew Gunder. Capitalism and Underdevelop-
    ment in Latin America. New York: Monthly
    Review Press, 1967.

_____. "The Varieties of Land Reform." Whither
    Latin America?. Edited by Huberman & Sweezy.
    New York: Monthly Review Press, 1963.

Gordon, Lincoln. A New Deal For Latin America: The
    Alliance for Progress (Cambridge: Harvard
    University Press, 1963).

Instituto Brasileiro de Reforma Agrária. Estatuto
    da Terra. Lei No. 4,504 de 30 de novembro de
    1964. Departamento de Imprensa Nacional.

_____. Decreto No. 55,891 de 31 de março de 1965.
    Regulamenta o Capítulo I de Título I e a seção
    III do Capítulo IV do Titulo II do Estatuto
    da Terra.

_____. Decreto No. 56,792 de 26 de agôsto de
    1965. Regulamenta o Capítulo I de Título III
    do Estatuto da Terra.

_____. Instrução Especial IBRA No. 1, 1965.
    Regulamenta dispositivos do Decreto No. 55,891
    e do Decreto No. 56,792 sobre o Zoneamento do
    Pais, Zonas Típicas e Módulos de Imóveis
    Rurais, os Cadastros a serem realizados pelo
    IBRA e a Tributação de Terra previsto no
    Estatuto da Terra.

_____. "Módulo." Cadernos do IBRA, Vol. II, No.
    1. Rio de Janeiro: IBRA. 1967.

_____. "A estrutura agrária brasileira." Dados
    preliminares, Vol. I. Rio de Janeiro: IBRA.
    1967.

Leite, Edgard Texeira. "O problema da terra no
    Brasil," Revista de Geografia, (April-June,
    1959), 127-146.

Nabuco, Lopes. Ensaio sobre alimentacão regional.
     Maceió: Edição do Departamento Estadual de
     Cultura, 1962.

Nascimento, N. "O camponês no norte do Paraná,"
     Revista Brasiliense, XLI (May-June, 1962),
     123-128.

_____. "A justiça e a reforma agrária," Revista
     Brasiliense, XXXIX (January-February, 1962),
     119-123.

Nicholls, W. H. & Paiva, R. M. "The Structure and
     Productivity of Brazilian Agriculture,"
     Journal of Farm Economics, XXXXVII (May,
     1965), 347-361.

Oberg, Kalervo. "The Marginal Peasant in Rural
     Brazil," Papers in Applied Anthropology. A
     Report Prepared by the United States
     Operations Mission. Rio de Janeiro: 1965.

Paixão, Moacyr. "Elementos da questão agrária,"
     Revista Brasilense, XXIV (September-October,
     1959), 51-73.

Prado Caio, Jr. "O estatuto do trabalhador,"
     Revista Brasiliense, XXXXVII (May-June, 1963).

Rodriges, Lincoln Monteiro. Tendências da reforma
     agrária no Brasil. Rio de Janeiro; Minis-
     terio da Agricultura, Serviço do Informação
     Agrícola, Setor Grafico, 1964. (Originally
     M.Sc. thesis, University of Wisconsin,
     Madison.)

Schulman, Samuel. "The Colono System in Latin
     America," Rural Sociology, XX, 1 (1955),
     34-40.

Smith, T. Lynn (ed). Agrarian Reform in Latin
     America. New York: Alfred A. Knopf, 1965.

Sommerfeld, Raynard M. Tax Reform and the Alliance
     for Progress. Austin: University of Texas
     Press. 1966.

United Nations, Department of Economic and Social
     Affairs. Progress in Land Reform: 1st
     Report. New York: United Nations, 1954.

_____. Progress in Land Reform: 4th Report.
      New York: United Nations, 1966.

Warriner, Doreen. Landlords and Peasants: Land
      Reform in Principle and Practice. Oxford
      University Press, 1968.

ABOUT THE AUTHORS

ARMIN K. LUDWIG, Associate Professor of Geography at Colgate University, graduated from Ball State University in 1952 and received his Ph.D. in geography from the University of Illinois in 1962. Since 1956 he has spent much time in field research in Brazil, working under grants from the Social Science Research Council, the Dupont Foundation, the Colgate Research Council, and the Agricultural Development Council. Working in Brazil with Dr. Robert L. Carmin of the University of Illinois in 1956, Dr. Ludwig participated in a study of the Goiás frontier, the region of Brazil's new capital, Brasília. In 1966 Dr. Ludwig published "The Planning and Creation of Brasília: Toward a New and Unique Brazilian Regional Environment?" in New Perspectives of Brazil, edited by Eric Baklanoff.

HARRY W. TAYLOR is Associate Professor of Geography at the University of Western Ontario. He was graduated in 1954 from West Chester State College and received his Ph.D. in geography from the University of Illinois in 1962. He researched his Ph.D. dissertation in Brazil in 1956-57 and 1961 and returned there in 1964 to update this work, at the invitation of Professor Ary Franca of the University of São Paulo's Institute of Geography. The Social Science Research Council supported Dr. Taylor's research in 1967-68 on Brazilian agrarian change. Dr. Taylor's previous publications include "Uma região produtora de sorgo nos Estados Unidos" in Boletim Paulista de Geografia and "Race and Population Patterns in Trinidad" in Annals of the Association of American Geographers.